IMPRESSIONS OF REALITY

Jean-Yves Solinga

FIRST EDITION

Little Red Tree Publishing, LLC,
635 Ocean Avenue, New London, CT 06320

Previous works:

Clair-Obscur of the Soul (2008)
Clair-obscur de l'âme [in French] (2008)
In the Shade of a Flower (2009)
Landscape of Envies (2010)
Words Made of Silk (2011)

Copyright © 2013 Jean-Yves Solinga

All rights are reserved under International and Pan-American Copyright Conventions. Except for brief passages quoted in a newspaper, magazine, radio or television review, no part of this book may be reproduced in any form or by any means, electronic or mechanical, including photocopying and recording, or by any information storage and retrieval system, without permission in writing from the publisher.

Layout and Cover Design: Michael Linnard
Text in Minion Pro, Trajan Pro and Ariel.

First Edition, 2013, manufactured in USA
1 2 3 4 5 6 7 8 9 10 LSI 19 18 17 16 15 14 13

Front cover painting, *Impression, soleil levant* by Claude Monet

Photographs of Jean-Yves on page xiii taken by Elaine Solinga and page 133 taken by Katie Norman. Copyright for both photos is held by Jean-Yves Solinga.

Painting of a Provençal vineyard on page 8, reproduced by kind permission of Jeannette Olson.

All other paintings that appear in this book are in the public domain and attributed individually.

Library of Congress Cataloging-in-Publication Data

Solinga, Jean-Yves
  Impressions of Reality / Jean-Yves Solinga. -- 1st ed.
    p. cm.
  Includes glossary and index.
  ISBN 978-1-935656-24-1 (pbk. : alk. paper)
  I. Title.
  PS3612.A58565S77 2013
  811'.6--dc23
                        2013018801

Little Red Tree Publishing LLC
635 Ocean Avenue,
New London Connecticut 06320
www.littleredtree.com

Contents

Foreword by Michael Linnard — vii
Introduction by Jean-Yves Solinga — ix

This Side of Illusion — 2
James Dean's Tee Shirt — 4
Cinecittà — 6
Provence: L'Arlésienne — 7
Mont Sainte-Victoire (French) — 9
Mont Sainte-Victoire (English) — 10
Beethoven's Universe — 11
Abstraction — 12
Saint Martin and the Donkey — 13
Holiday Meal Chemistry — 14
The Beagle and the Kitten — 15
Barnyard Noises — 16
Surprise — 17
Wishing Otherwise — 18
Small Things — 19
I've Got to Die Like Sinatra — 20
Of Purple Rain and Other Things — 21
Knowing too Much — 22
Cold Indifference — 23
Dying Tendrils — 24
University Bull Sessions and the Universe — 25
Once Upon a Time in the Future — 27
The Cathedral and the Meter Maid — 28
Turing's Cathedral — 29
Slow Dancing — 31
Warm Sand — 33

Verbal Architecture of Past Happiness	34
Bluish Marble	35
Google Earth and Heartbreak	36
The End of Everything	37
Total Recall	38
Sounds of Silence in the Kitchen	39
Denied	41
Inconvenient	42
Amplification	43
Replaced	44
Patches of Meaning	45
Different Endings	46
Priorities	47
ICU	48
Gods and Codes	50
Yellow Lights	51
Past Third and Going Home	53
Custer's Last Stand	55
Natural Laws and Gods	56
Dreamscape	57
A Good Start	59
One Size Fits All	60
Ideals and Fairytales	61
Candide (Revisited)	62
Pâté de campagne and Laissez-faire	63
Of Guano and Human Progress	64
The Pyramid Builder II	65
Pavlovian Sounds	66
Abnormal in a Normal World	67
Of Instinctive Nurturing	68
Africa	69
Compartmentalization	70
Reparations: Camus and Capital Punishment	71
Obscenity	73
Temerity	75
Splendid Fragility	76
Number 174517	78
Beautiful Ship	80
Le beau navire	81
The Ice Cream Truck	82

Avatar	83
Digitized Bebris	84
Love Molecule	85
Loved Trait	87
Indice aimé	88
No Longer of his World	89
Men and Moths	90
The Boxer and the Sparrow	91
Sightless Images	92
An Eternal Second	93
Une seconde éternelle	95
Not Forgotten	96
The Name That Must Not Be Said	98
The End of Simplicity	100
Into Dust	101
En poussière	103
Parallels	105
Lace	106
La dentelle	107
Shaping the Future	108
Façonner le futur	109
Counter Currents	110
The Effect of a Butterfly	111
L'effet d'un papillon	112
Immortal Embers	113
The Life of a Bubble	115
Light and Flesh	118
Glossary	119
Index of Titles and First Lines	127
About the Author	133

Foreword

It is a rare occurrence indeed when a publisher begins to write a foreword to the sixth full-length book of poetry from the same author. Such is the case with Jean-Yves Solinga's book, *Impressions of Reality*. Very few poets write such quantity, rightfully earning the accolade "enviably prolific" from Christie Williams in his comments on the back cover. Being prolific, in and of itself, is certainly praiseworthy but then there is the question of quality, which is without doubt self-evident.

In Jean-Yves' first book *Clair-Obscur of the Soul* (2008) I wrote in the foreword that I had enthusiastically accepted his first manuscript for publication, "...because of its intensity, lyricism and insight into the essence of what it is to be human, in fact beyond and through to the heart and soul." Nothing in this book undermines or diminishes that assessment, in fact it has increased. Therefore, what we have here is a new book of wonderfully crafted poetry that embraces a forgotten past through to the political implications of modernity.

With his finely-tuned sense of what it is, not only, to be a poet, but an artist, and his customary third-person voice full of didactic possibilities, Jean-Yves is fearless. No subject is beyond reach, and few are omitted here. Jean-Yves translates and subsumes his art into each poem with such mellifluous grace that it hides the multi-layers of meaning, complexity and technique involved. We are left merely to savor—as if tasting an excellent French wine—and enjoy the moments created within each poem.

I highly recommend this book to those in search of a new vision—an impression—to interpret the past, present and future existential reality we all inhabit and at times struggle to comprehend.

Michael Linnard
New London, CT. April 2013

The envious author, in front of the Château de Montgeoffroy near Angers, France. This castle, finished just before the French Revolution, was spared the destructive results of history. More importantly, its working kitchens still showing its entire original copperware, are regularly used by its owners for intimate meals for their thirty or forty friends. (Photo taken by Elaine Solinga)

Introduction

The wide range of themes in this book reminded me of a remark, concerning my analytical process, made earlier in my career. "Impressionistic," it was said to be. This was at the time of preparation for my dissertation when I knew that strict linear analysis should have been at a premium. Some of my earlier attempts at writing about the Maghreb [North Africa] had been more akin to lyrical prose. By nature, I was not comfortable in the colder depths of topics: Being more at ease in the surface imagery and angular relationships rather than in background precision. Could it be that the respectable facets of this expansive term were used as a double-edged qualifier for my approach? Was "Impressionistic" meant to emphasize a palpable sensitivity in the patina of my work? Was it unwillingly prophetic: In the way Parisian critiques would learn to feel about Monet's apparent lack of interest in details focusing instead on the overall effect? No unlike the way the sun comes in and out and the lack of precision of the boats in *Impression, soleil levant* on the front cover. Thus making the result emotionally more lasting than the geometric precision of any photograph.

At any rate, facing the freedom of the first blank page of a new book of poetry seems to continually reinforce and to satisfy this personal leaning. The result, I think, produced this seemingly chaotic spread of themes in my subjects: From the ethereal to the commonly and solidly real. It is also behind the choice of title of the book: *Impressions of Reality*. These poems are the result of the cross-fertilization of the landscapes of things and people on me and, in return, the effect of my very presence among them ("This Side of Illusion" [p.2]). It is also a respectful and loving reference to my primordial visit to the Musée Marmottan in Paris when I saw first-hand this glorious canvas. A remark made to my publisher, Michael Linnard, led us to put this quintessential human statement of timeless beauty on the cover.

As indicated by the choice for my first poems, such as "This Side of Illusion" [p.2], the universe of the technique of film-making or story telling affected my formative years and set the tone for dealing with my presence in front of perceived multiple worlds of reality: Worlds, in this instance, on both side of the giant movie screens of my youth ("James Dean's Tee Shirt" [p.4]). I thus constructed a personal vision of the relationship between me and my written text. This gap is often the basis of what constructs my idea of fiction as used in my poems. I readily enter unrestrained into this 'fictional buffer' in order to wander in what is the 'writer-text' dimension: All the while applying a concept of poetry as a genre that is wide enough to take in a variety of issues: Hence the subtext of Reality in the qualifier of the book title as seen in the tradition of societal, temporal topics found in Hugo, Lamartine, Alfred de Vigny or Léopold Senghor.

This writer-text space is built with an amalgam of various levels of realities, surrealities or pastiches. There exist of course snippets of absolute temporal moments experienced, read or related that I include in whole or in part: "Number 174517" [p.77] (A tattooed concentration number), "ICU" [p.48] (Observations in an Intensive Care Unit), "Compartmentalization" [p.70] (Governmental Medical Studies Accounts of Cold War nuclear fallout on American civilian populations around test sites) for instance. These historical moments are then pasted in my choice of state-of-being sequences, nightmarish abysses or paradisiac euphory that I blend with the paint of poetry in order to give continuity or to fill gaps for unknown details. I therefore give myself the literary option of enriching the ambiance of a poem. In this calculus, some poems come, at times, the closest to imitating the verbal vastness of the prose genre. Indeed, I like to think of some of my poems as having the descriptive geometry of asymptotes. That is: Coming infinitesimally close to the verbal density of prose but never touching it, never crossing it: Never losing, for instance, the poetic descriptive identity of Charles Baudelaire's poetic prose. At its most effective, I would like my poetry to be a world of the transparency of reality of the moment. At times during the writing process, I literally do not know where the poem is going, *Les mots appellent les mots*: Words call out for words. This is why I quote this passage of *The Ecstasy of Illusion* by Jonathan Lethem in the marginal note of "This Side of Illusion." "I began writing in order to arrive into the company of those whose company meant more to me than any other." I hasten to add that in my case, I mean all parts of things and persons of my poetic "company." While some of the poems are grounded in a measure of truth or reality, as I see them, the ultimate weapon of poetry over straight prose is its distillation through the fine mesh of some sort of inevitable lyricism. In this vein, I hope that even my most *Realpolitik*-oriented poetry contains this particular element: ("Reparations: Camus and Capital Punishment" [p.71], not a typical poetic subject). These intrusions of history and science do give an uncharacteristic hard edge to some poems.

The general perception is that the 'author-text separation' is often assumed to be smaller in lyrical poetry: This, as a result of the sometimes intimate or personal tone of the pieces. It is therefore proper to restate my position from previous prefaces in reference to questions [more particularly asked of poets] that go along the line of: "Did this really happen to you?" Why not ask then: "Did you ever witness or partake in murders" from crime story novelists?

On the other hand, there are indeed poems in this collection that are the result of biographical or autobiographical situations and I openly give them markers that make this obvious; a reference to a family member, a family event or historical character. But in the poem "Beautiful Ship" [p.80], about my holding onto my father's shoulders as he swam in the Mediterranean Sea, I still take liberties as to details and leave out a later unpleasant unrelated scare during the same day. So, even in this, one of my more non-fictional poems, I have toyed with reality. I have selected the more positive pieces of my past based on my favorite memories of youth. Another example is the poem "Different Ending" [p.46], about two boys during World War Two. It is based on family lore: My brother was indeed one of the boys. But I had to make up all the details of the story and leave out again some even more heart ranching ones. Still, the vital power of the poem resides in its overall sadness: That of imposing war conditions on children. And yes, sadly, the other boy did disappear in the 'fog' of war. In "Splendid Fragility" [p.76] about Jorge Semprùn and his concentration camp experience, I take only the smallest snippets of his autobiographical book and build my own imagery around it. This poem, dedicated to this French-Spanish writer, turned out to be one of the more difficult and time-consuming to finish. And in spite of an understandable unease with the topic, it was a surprisingly satisfying endeavor after the fact. Furthermore, as an attempt to present to the reader with the equivalent of an antidote for the malignancy of the subject, I concluded the poem with this splendidly fragile word: "Life."

As a rule, I guide my poetry away from the circumstantial, the personal, the autobiographical. It is not from an overdeveloped sense of modesty but rather in favor of the unbridled freedom given to my writing by a more unrestricted palette of emotions, persons and places: As it was recommended in the French Seventeenth Century Classical vein.

I continue to find a good portion of my socially and politically charged poems in the expected places such as thoughtful articles; but also at times through accidental observations such as a refreshingly unencumbered urban university setting at Spring break as in "Love Molecule" [p.85], or it could be the recall of an event from my past that becomes the basic structure for a poem with a larger topic on which I had previously been frustratingly laboring. This is the case with "University Bull Sessions and the Universe" [p.25] where I conflate two themes: Mankind's apparent loneliness in the Universe and the often 'foggy', weird, warm solidarity and camaraderie of university dorm life that we fondly remember many years later.

I have to acknowledge my emotional preference for writing lyrical poetry: Even if it is about unhappy, even tragic emotions ("Men and Moths" [p.90]) and its reference to Bizet's *Carmen*. Nevertheless, even in the case of burning lyricism, I prefer hints of universality and keep a measured distance from the text "Avatar"[p.83], "Lace"[p.106]. I do not want my lyricism to become uncomfortable or circumstantial. It is Montaigne, among others, who searched in the individual for timeless or universal elements.

Not surprisingly, powerful aspects of lyrical poetry are gathered by voyeuristic observations of surrounding personal events. Yes! It is what artists do! They mine people around them to give themselves material for inspiration. Some of my lyrical poems reinforce the anecdotal wisdom that you open yourself to all sorts of pain if you dabble with love. Some of these are heartbreakingly sad in the matter of Jacques Brel: "Not Forgotten" [p.96], "Into Dust" [101], "Sightless Images" [92]. The Rolling Stones said it with the back-up of an angelic children choir: "You don't always get what you want."

Poetry is at one of its best when it can be both instructive and beautiful as when displaying the haunting echoes of love: "Love Molecule" [p.85] which is an ode to what still remains of the dignity of the self-awareness of human senses and emotions in a world of the ever-increasing omnipresence and omniscience of computers. As an optimistic nod to the future, I dedicated "The Life of a Bubble" [p.115] to my grandchildren Noëlle and Luc.

I want to thank my wife Elaine, my son Robert, his wife Elizabeth, my daughter Nicole and her husband Marc and a circle of warm friends for giving me a cocoon of emotional comfort that has made my life a gift and my wine more enjoyable.

For his steadfast friendship, guidance and indulgence for my numerous marginal notes to my poems, I thank once more Michael Linnard of Little Red Tree Publishing.

Jean-Yves Solinga
Gales Ferry
May, 2013

A vision of vacuity. "A bar at the folies bèrgere" (1882) by Edouard Manet

Images from the inexhaustible rich fertility of the artist's reconstruction of reality

Images de la riche et inépuisable fertilité chez l'artiste dans sa reconstruction de la réalité

Monet's artistic vision of a new technological reality ("Gare Saint Lazare" (1877)).

IMPRESSIONS
OF
REALITY

This side of illusion

Darken world of unreeling pops and hisses.
Finalized comfort of last cough from squeaky seats.

Tantalizing undressing of preparatory layers
Of cartoons and world news,
Wetting appetites for center stage big feature.

Cocoon of cinder block walls
In cocoon-city.

Tabernacle of blood-red curtains
Opening unto 'cycloptic' pasty whiteness of screen.

Antithetical temporary existence
In world of tortuous stories,
Unconventional cultures and leanings.

Wild beasts and wilder inner thoughts
Exploding on the screen.

The possible and its opposite co-existing
In dreamy incestuous realities.

Avidly drinking, in visual elixirs, intoxicating potions
Made of surprising titillations from so-called moral tales.

 Escapist germs from the Petri dish of the human condition:
Those found in the hardness of realities.
And hidden ones of children's tales.

Hoping till the end for that happy ending,
Disappearing at the rate of sweetness of Bazooka bubble gum:

Quasimodo somehow never waking up to the sounds of swallows
Flying through the cathedral's towers:
His distorted body having been left to his nightmarish past.

Steadfastly trying to impose a child's world

Where the green-stone beauty of Esmeralda could transform any repulsion
Into an outward mirror of human worth and happiness.

Construction and deconstruction of the real and imagined.
Of the now and the forever.

Imagining beyond the possible and warranted
That other side of imagination.

Finding ourselves back on the velour of our theatre,
Sitting on this side of the screen,

Prologue to the long walk back home
Among the dull familiarities of the city street.

Homage to childhood escapism and passion of watching movies on huge theater screens. And thoughts on the physical divide that used to exist in large movie theatres where these screens acted as a symbolic barrier between realities.

As well as this from the New York Times Book Review *(November 27, 2011) The quote is taken from the author in* The Ecstasy of influence *by Jonathan Lethem. "I began writing in order to arrive into the company of those whose company meant more to me than any other."*

James Dean's Tee Shirt

Out-of-body experience...
Into a truly extraterrestrial world out of Africa.

Emotional flight...
Stimulated by foreign ingredients
Of bizarre objects and apparently unrestricted, untamed spaces and places
Made of gaudy colorized plastics and transparent, inorganic table tops.

Cosmic pull...
 Away from the immediate surroundings
Made of the unstable mixture of modern cars, decrepit donkeys,
Gasoline fumes and gigantic flies hovering over street fecal matter.

Worlds and cultures...
Colliding in this Maghrebian accelerator:
The result of overlapping puritanical jellabas and Dior understated sexuality.

But nothing could have prepared him for the blunt impact...
Of this primordial scream of adolescent pain among the
free flowing whiskey sours;
The quasi-medieval streets outside the movie house
And the gratuitous elegance... The wasteful tempting imagery of flying
hunks of metal;
The conflict with the Lilliputian scale of his world
And the surrealistic tortuous endlessness of school hallways
Inhabited by a special breed
Endowed with visceral, brown bedroom glances
Full of strange teenage intensity:

All of this Brave New World of things yet to come.

Wild-eyed stupor, in the conspiring darkness of the theatre,
Fed by the flowing genesis of pubescence:
Resonating in the still awkward flesh,
Looking, with envy, at the secret codes displayed on the super-human screen.

All of it magically and internally captured,
In the palpitating breaths under the cotton of the gleaming white tee-shirt:

Tantalizingly exposed in the open slit
Made by the silky Cardinal hue of the jacket.

Impact of Rebel without a Cause. *It was the last American movie seen in the 'self-contained world' of the big screens of the past. It took place in Morocco before my expatriation to America (1959). This movie was a sort of rite of passage.*
Nota Bene: With the usual biographical poetic license.

Cinecittà

Evils of twisted minds and times:
Constructed celluloid characters forced upon us and our souls
Through our eyes.

Sadistic voyages allowing us to wander freely
Into the perverted corners of the impossible.

Unrestricted thoughts turned into cinematic realities:
Filthy asylums of inhumanity and the de-humanizing.

The joyless ride of outsized egos of evil
Guiding us through the tunnel of tears.

Scenes reaching to the asymptotes
To the very border between agony and laughter,

Thus playing dangerously with the ingredients
Making the unacceptable... acceptable by its normalized omnipresence.

Infliction of pain and anguish to feed the beast and bestial.
Institutionalization of the gratuitous and instant Kafkaesque injustice.

The ultimate goal...
Making the reign of meaninglessness of the absurd:
Repetitive... Concrete... And intimate.
Turning all of us into hopeless children of Sisyphus.

And then... and then...
 This moral tale... From the so-called dumb universe:
Worthy of the archives of the Cinecittà...

A planet-size diamond... Worth of guilt.

Inspired by the surrealistic imagery of such artists as Lina Wermuller and Frederico Felllini about the inhumanity of societies and wars. As well as speculation upon a would be forgotten script in the dusty drawers of Cinecittà from these two directors. Here we have news of this grandiose, outlandish absurdity, a planet-size diamond, speculated upon by physicists. What a visual and moral tale to counter-balance the inhumanity inflicted in the search of the 'blood diamonds of Africa!'

Provence : l'Arlésienne Suite, Farandole et Carillon

Essences of petals. Extracts of sunlight.
Landscapes in shades of romantic breezes and imperious Mistral.
August explosions of obedient sunflowers.

Hilltops dreamingly floating as curved resonances
among carillons calls from inside flowery campaniles.

Oils from centenary trees clinging to cracked barks.
Pastoral of white spots climbing sheepishly toward olive grove shade.

Solar ecstasy extracted from lowly black musical notes in eternal language
that would be heard long after his molecular silence.

Did Bizet know upon his last concept of any human concept,
In that last moment and for the glory of the rest of us,
That he would continue to exist in the fleeting but eternal moments
of violin strings trembling under the archet's touch?

Or in the metallic solidity of the French horns,
And the palpitating sanguinity of the tambourin?

Could he still hear the elasticity of his music
Well before the unyielding inevitable blackness took over?

Brittle feuilleté of sounds among glorious trumpet solidity.
Gentle layers of vibrato and the mosaic of echoes of kingly marches
under the majesty of pastoral bells.

Nature's nuptials of distillate of solar world with the cool granite cobble stones:
Witnessed by stubborn medieval field walls.

Godly ability, through his mere human inspired craving,
To transpose vibrations of the heart into tonalities of the soul.

Brass masculinity answered, note by rhythmic note,
with a counter-current of fluid tenderness from the vaporous pulsing of strings.

Tiptoe of flutes joyfully spreading the powdery clouds of lavender
over the burnt earth alive with nervous cicadas.

Distant bluish waves of ghostly jagged mountain tops
Giving reference in the severe crystalline Mediterranean skies.

Musical reconstruction of this privileged ancient landscape,
Home now to the families of gods who came to rest after their descent from
Olympus to reflect on mankind:
And now, spending the rest of their languorous eternities among us
In the perfume of maritime pines.

Homage to Georges Bizet

Painting of a Provençal vineyard by Jeannette Olson

Mont Sainte-Victoire

Il existe un chemin près de Marseille.
Il vit sur une colline face au soleil
Et dans le regard d'un petit garçon tenant la main de son père.

Il essaie encore de cacher sa terre rougeâtre
Au milieu du vert translucide des pins maritimes.

Son paysage se définit en nuances de cascades en pastel,
En contrastes de surfaces et de textures verticales,

De collines silencieuses faites de granite et de cigales amoureuses,
De la fraîcheur sèche des ombres,

De la présence insupportable de la chaleur
Et du parfum aigre-doux des essences d'aiguilles de pins
Qui suintent doucement leur hommage à l'univers :

Incorporant de futurs souvenirs
Pour les fortunés qui y passeront à leur tour.

Du poème en anglais inspiré par la couverture du livre Landscape of Envies [2010] de Jean-Yves Solinga montrant le tableau de Mont Sainte-Victoire de Paul Cézanne du Courtland Institute Galleries à Londres.

Mont Sainte-Victoire

There is a path near Marseille.
It lives on a hill facing the Sun
And in the glance of a little boy holding his father's hand.

It is still trying to hide its reddish soil
Among the transparent green of the Maritime Pines.
The landscape defines itself in shades of cascading pastels,

Contrasting vertical surfaces and textures
Of silent granite hills and amorous Cicadas,
The dry coolness of the shade,

The overwhelming presence of the heat
And the sweet acrid scent of the essence of pine needles
Gently oozing their reverence of the World.

Instilling future memories
For the fortunate taking their turn passing through.

From Landscape of Envies (2010)

Beethoven's Universe

Seemingly flat world of photographic stillness.
Remnants of summer hours, stony silence of things, people
and petrified moments.

Straining to see just the beginning of a smile on her lips,
Stopped in its track by the speed of the shutter.

Photograph apparently constructed of silent echoes
Answered by reluctant echoes among the stiffened coffee vapors
Next to arrested reach for the sugar.

And especially... Stopped on the glossy paper...
Her laughter.
The one following his cognac induced remark.

None of these moments, that make moments precious,
Could be rehydrated from the celluloid desert
In the casual quiet of a family album.

But like Beethoven's envious glance upon the hard yet willing piano keys
He could turn that hint of ivory in her smile
Into a rhapsody of sensuous sounds.

Thus recreating from this outdated and unassuming treasure
The magic of a voice surrounded by divine silence.

Beethoven, having become functionally deaf, could recreate in his mind the sounds of his notes on the music sheet. And thus for some, the echoes of a loved one's voice can still be heard among the silence of the mind upon looking at just an old photograph.

Abstraction

Layered sheets of brittle lithium whiteness
Shooting into celestial ink.

Dagger made of plates aimed at smitten urban gods.
Construct made of architectural hope and arrogance.

Artistic magic fashioning into metallic solidity
The molecular twist of living vines.

Among her envious sisters
Pagan cathedral to beauty and height.

Inspired by Max Weber's "Abstraction" (1913). Painting of the Chrysler building in New York City in the New Britain, Connecticut Museum of American Art.

Saint Martin and the Donkey

Humanity tries to decipher knowledge
Wherever pieces of it seem to present themselves:
At times leading to the enjoyment of living:

Druids listening to the magical vibrations
From wrinkled leaves and impatient streams.

Baudelaire telling us of the beauty of coded cadences
Found in multi layered idioms made of corresponding images and meanings.

But at other times, we cloud the air of university halls
With a strict regimen of bitter medicines from frigid philosophies:

Right... Wrong. Justice.
Or the perversions of them all.

And then...
And then we encounter this donkey:
Having supported with proletariat equanimity
The clerical derrière of medieval eminence,

This marvelously daring, hungry and proverbially stupid beast,
Poorest among the poorest animals,

Eating his way to a glorious discovery:
For the universal betterment of mankind.

Tradition has it that Bishop Saint Martin of Tours, France [316-397], interested in winemaking, had come from his native Hungary with vines which he then planted in Touraine. Upon a visitation of his vineyards the Bishop tethered his donkey near his fields whereupon the hungry animal proceeded to eat some of the leaves. The effected vines turned out to be the most productive of the lot. Local folklore credits this incident for the now standard practice of pruning vines and hence better wines.

Holiday Meal Chemistry

Smirks of disapproval from the rightist corner of the clan
About white or dark meat.

More unease from the 'Puritans' corner
About the muscular thighs on the bird.

An Aunt's green thumb was good for a few minutes,
As well as the escalating monthly cost of cable connections.
A detour into latest familial happy and unhappy hospital experiences:

Then…
What safer topic then that of the straw man of office miseries?

When an innocent follow-up question
About a particular change in husband's firm

And its only answer by the church-choir like response
From the assembled… Of the name…

Of the then in-coming secretary,

Source of nights on the couch
And slight hesitation of the knife into the turkey's breast.

The adage is for not talking about religion and politics at family gatherings; but the list is not comprehensive.

The beagle and the kitten

Off the side of the road and far from kindness,
Dropped away from human embrace into black asphalt hardness,

Well away from salvation and the cottoned blanket of decency,
Left in the unpredictable mortal calculus of road kill,

With no gods of any specie looking down
And only the steel belted whining
Answering the frightened puzzlement of animal glances…

… A giant protective crescent curve took form
In the belly of the diminutive animal

And did what no dusty books or beliefs needed to impose:

Extend true human warmth.

Inspired by a real event of a beagle and kitten abandoned by the side of a highway: The beagle was found protecting the kitten with his belly.

As well as a reflection on the thought by the writer and Shoa survivor Jorge Semprún who… [Paraphrasing]… said the horrors that he had witnessed were ironically 'human' since they had been perpetrated by human beings. To call them inhuman acts was a misnomer according to Semprún. Indeed these actions had their very sources in humanity.

Barnyard noises

Lessons to be learned and wisdom to be gathered
Among feathered animal posturing in fecal matter.

Thinking about its troubling double ganger under Federal domes
With bloated double breasted congressional members.

Lessons to be learned and wisdom to be gathered
In pathetic line up of belligerent urban youth at some random street address:
Crowing their muscular strength and displaying their virility.

Both groups passing off guttural noises as communication.
Intimidation being the currency of political and street values.

Illusion of happiness in self-assigned political power.
Or swagger of walk in front of gang members:
Both equal in their ultimate sterile triviality.

Makes you wonder what sort of world would instead have been
If evolutionary survival had been given to the gentlest:

Giving us indeed the best of the best of worlds.

Upon listening to two crowing roosters trying to outdo each other.
And, reflection on the evolution of mankind and Voltaire stance on tolerance.

Surprise!

Public apparitions:
Iconic disheveled hair and telling bloodshot eyes.
Sharp ideas and clear vision after foggy nights.

Furious debates furiously held.
Limitless arguments succinctly presented.

Minutia of points of view defended.
Opponents intellectually slain.

Imperceptible smirk married to steely tone.
Impeccable grammar reinforced by perfect etymology.

Unfolding of full panoply
Of nobility of Enlightened Philosophic lineage.

Divine presence of television lights.
Secularity of glare toward amazed admirers.

All this worldly artifice
All of it… Now well behind.

This heart and mind preparing and prepared for the ultimate
Of ultimate of moments:

It would be IT… and then nothing:

Leaving behind last images of earthly pleasures
That had existed in moments of exalting human solidarity:

Those anchored in the multicolored solidity of life and living
Fading into the inevitable richness of black.

In "Afterlife Debate: David Hitchen and Sam Harris versus David Wolpe and Bradley Artson Sahvit" about the possibility on an afterlife, the confirmed Atheist Hitchen stated "… I like surprises…", if he were to find some afterlife after his own death. [On YouTube]

Wishing Otherwise

Bright of mind… Short of stature.
Reasonably brave of heart… Slim of muscles.

Line-up at office party… And jostled by men,
Overlooked by women.

Prized degree in hand… But caveat about diminutive height.

Obliged to taller friendly colleagues
For vital introductory hand shake in networking settings.

Mind you,
Not as bad as anti-Semitism, sexism or racism
Not as unfelling as homophobia,

But distressful nevertheless
Upon return to favorite armchair and late-night television show.

Bank vice-president during a job interview: "I should tell you that I think your small height could hurt you professionally in a large meeting setting."

Small Things

Wrought iron chairs and tables:
Yard sale attempt at elegance.

Quasi European atmosphere:
At New World attempt.

Regulars attending with regular no lettuce habits.
Freshness of fish inquiries from overheated summer wanderers.

Small place for quiet large coffee and larger oatmeal cookies.
Mumbles and grumbles of acknowledgment:
From voice behind the New York Times.

Discreet tangential glances at expensive-clad Levies derrières
Of A.O.C. Châteaux grade middle-age women.

The significance of little things at work
That makes blank glances at watch less blank.

It was not much...
It really didn't know of its role in the Universe:

But it left one less obstacle to its consciousness.

In the window of tiny New England village establishment: "The management is sorry to announce that we will close permanently next week."

I've Got to Die Like Sinatra

Seemingly unforced innate fluidity.
Godly blend of virile baritone vibrations,
Accompanied by sensual mystery of disincarnated vocals.

Swooning vibrato of surprising femininity
Emanating from impeccably cut midnight-dark suits
Echoed by the smoky architecture of enunciation.

Flawless armor made of polished cloth and demeanor
Covering fragility of slender flesh and ego.

Sorcery of rich amalgam of adolescent glance,
Sprinkled with bird-of-prey marbly-blue crystalline severity.

No blanched hospital sheets or tubing.
No last second labored aspiration.
No bodily secretions entering this iconic universe.

Like an old decorated Spartan fighter
Answering the intimate call to cross over to the eternal side,
He must have walked... Solitary and proud as ever...

... Away from the voyeuristic eyes of the common...
Into his proper share of the Elysian fields,

To die the mythological death offered only to our divinities:

... To the oozing sexuality...

Of a heavenly chorus of black-silk clad alto-sopranos.

With references to Maroon 5, Mick Jagger and Frank Sinatra. The author has no knowledge of the circumstances of Mr. Sinatra's death and does not want to know: This is based on his still remaining iconic stage presence.

Of Purple Rain and Other Things

Androgynous undercurrent of sexuality.
Un-verbalized secrets of intimacy.

Power chords in filigreed harmony with restrained cadences.
Part of romantic equation of the richness of life
Found in complementary opposites.

Tenderness of kisses
And their unseen powers.

Entities touching at that precise point of contact,
Not unlike God's outstretched index to our index.

Knowledge of knowledge entrusted:
Everything that is everything passed on,

Among sweeping amplifications of Wagnerian swells,
From the plaintive cry of metallic strings,
Titillated to pounding exhaustion.

Feminine falsetto that will continue its resonance
As a virile echo at our hour of death:

Like a witness to what is truly the godly arrogance of Mankind…

A belief in the singularity of human passions.

Iconic kisses such as the ones in Charles Aznavour YouTube's version of "Tous les visages de l'amour" ["She" in the English version] and particularly by Prince's kiss on the cheek of his female guitarist at the end of the song "Purple Rain" from the movie of the same name.

Knowing too much

At the center of everything:
All knowing and all doing.

With fingers into the smallest minutia
And waving hands over grandiose projects.

Abrasive tone and harsher decisions.
Not amused by amusing things and people.

A serious man of puritanical bend.
No nonsense spouse with multiple ex-spouses.

Left now to the sum of his mindless flesh
In a mass of unconscious peace.

Multiple reactions upon recognizing a once extremely driven and opinionated executive quietly sitting in a corner of the Alzheimer "memory pavilion" of a hospital.

Cold indifference

Sparkles in a human mind
In a very human instant
Of the grandeur of its human condition,

Reflecting on its place and the weakness of its place:
Spreading contagious arrogance of its pretensions
In smart corners of doomed defiance.

Could dumb and deaf things be
Grudgingly envious of such poignant delusions:

That of imposing a human landscape
On topographies of imperiously petrified…
Immeasurably cold… Indifference?

Reflection on the lyricism of these lines from Lawrence M. Krauss describing the lonely scenario of mankind's status in Things. In an article by Ann Levin for the Associated Press: "For Krauss, the prospect of a godless universe is 'invigorating' not scary. It motivates us to draw meaning from our actions," [Krauss] writes, "and to make the most of our brief existence in the sun."

Dying Tendrils

A certain pride still on display,
Basking in memories of her hours in the sun

She...
Lets us, on this solar side of her escaping year,
Glimpse at golden voyeuristic shadows of sensual sinuosity.

Translucent fibers of a fragile past
Holding on to once pulsating veins:
The ones that had nursed a world of seemingly endless lactating fertility

Schematic microcosm
Of a past shrunken to its last living molecules.

Visions in silhouettes...
Transparency...
And vanishing time.

Object of old desires and envies among all of her other companions.

Once all vibrant and pliable...
Now submissive in their dissolution in late summer brittle quivers.

Un-verbalized sadness staring at this tree.
Speechless human frustration facing both:

A disappearing and disappeared past
So elegantly captured in gentle plant-voices from an unpretentious universe.

Visions in silhouettes...
Transparency...
And vanishing time.

Visions of a late summer oak leaf.

University Bull Sessions and the Universe

A friendly slap on the back.
Sarcastic remark about inability with calculus:
Followed by invitation to 'review' session.

Off the cuff comments
About the draft. The war. Diseases of all types.

Undying bigotry and social injustices:
Like so much unstoppable seeping humidity into a cold cellar.

This bull session in the largest room of the freshmen dorm.
Complete with throw away comments meant as throw away statements:

Carrying the frustrations of negligible impact of our views
As so much paper bags from fast food tables.

And yet... And yet...

In a giant leap of ironic comparison
One of them could not help himself in interjecting
A random thought... About:

"This room. This group.
This university. And this world,
Floating with mankind aimlessly through space."

Asking his irritated dorm-mates to contemplate
Their diminutive status in the surrounding galactic spirals.

Imparting on the forced intimacy of the boozy conversation
The ironic gravitas, sincerity and poignancy of a greater humanism.

And yes... The magic...
The undeniable presence of reciprocal consciousness
Found in this fraternal setting of true friends and cheap beer.

Moments of touching solidarity
In the clanging steam-heat in this fourth floor room!

Something that astronauts of the deep future, will probably never encounter,
With their smart suits and smarter machines.

As they take their solitary walks outside their solitary spaceships
Incapable of recognizing the other tenants in the universe.

All of us will be on our respective sides:
Stage right and stage left,

All waiting and wanting for Godot to appear…
In the oppressive silence in this forest with falling trees.

Iconic question of a tree falling in a forest and no-one being there to hear it: What does it say about our human consciousness about others in the universe? Also inspired by futurists and astrophysicists who have stated their beliefs that even if some types of other consciousness exist, the statistical reality is that we may never come to be aware of one another because of the vastness of the Cosmos. Scientists furthermore predict that we would not recognize each other as sentient presences due to the enormous intellectual separation: Never becoming aware of the existence of others in the universe outside of our own.

Once upon a time… in the future

Molecular relationships and atomic-size egos.
Social circles restrained, during the voyage,
To the space between proteins beakers and sparkling electrodes.

Swirling pieces of life
Circling on wavelets of life supporting broths.

Destiny of precious cargo in the care of stainless pliers of obedient robots
The whole riding on programed sojourn toward specks of worlds
Somewhere out of this world.

One wonders whether, if once reconstituted,
This primordial soup of humanity will have carried within it enzymes
The memory of mankind's mortal flaws?

Forget Star Trek *and space voyagers in sexy outfits and steamy intimate close-up… only pieces of our DNA will be able to travel through space and time.*

"Do robots carry grudges?"[Repartee heard at a social activity]

The Cathedral and the Meter Maid

Properly scented rabbit pâté.
Blanquette de veau in silky sauce.

Balance of texture of cheese from contented local goats
Rare light red from Anjou, available with jaded abandonment.

Historic glass panes in dining room, giving sacramental note to meal.
Aggressively domed cobblestones, now imposing their medieval
heritage on stylish Stiletto heels.
Uneven venerable floors, remembering the footsteps of tired travelers
and haughty bishop.

Grande dame dressed in best gothic whitish regional stones:
Imposing genuine, profound respectability of culture;
Proudly unconcerned with its postcard quality setting.

A truly magical portico to a seemingly natural and uninterrupted past:
Except... For this smartly clad meter maid,
Attaching a note straight from contemporary Hell.

At the back of the venerable gothic "Cathédrale Saint-Maurice d'Angers," is a little square and an exquisite old restaurant. Depth of French culinary culture. Looking through the stain glass effect of the uneven glass of the restaurant into a tiny cobble stone square limited by the back of the cathedral and ancient houses. And then... admits a quasi-slip into a previous century the emotional and psychological dreamscape is invaded by a meter maid in the smart deep blue of officialdom: slipping parking tickets under the windshield wipers thus making for brusque historical dichotomy.

Turing's Cathedral: Lost Paradise

That snake had been there all the while
Despite our feigned trepidations, our uneasy conscience.

We had to understand. We always had to know.
We would never stop. We could not stop.

Reader of the coffee grounds of the gratuitous randomness.
Visionary of things beyond the quietude behaving numeration:
Turing wanted to see behind the proverbial curtain

Looking not for a divinity but rather play with the repetitive-divine in
the nature of things

Like the forbidden room in The Beauty and the Beast,
like all these scenes from the scary movies of our teen age years....

We had to go upstairs. We had to find that door.
We had to look for the lock: Fashion a key and turn it.

To the creaky opening of the door we see,
We capture, we drink in this Brave New World:
The last of all new worlds...

At least until the moment when the Universe will declare itself exhausted:
And do whatever exhausted universes do.

But until then... We will have dealt,
In an anxious Faustian bargain, interchangeable pieces of us
With their corresponding materiality in codes and silicon.

Entering into a replica of a Holy of Holies
Where we will come as close to the singularity of existence:
And its only value for us... the awareness of this existence.

Then... Sit for the rest of bio-engineered Time:
Realizing that curious thinkers, looking into the sparkling blackness of ancient Egyptian skies,
Were taking the first nibbles into that luscious apple.

The unquenchable human thirst to question since the iconic 'biblical' tree of knowledge.

This poem is inspired by a work by George Dyson about Alan Turing's "vision of a Universal Machine" and the type of computing that opened up the biological world to the world of numbers (DNA etc...) and the evolution of life itself.

A view of Paris before the Eiffel Tower. ("View of roofs of Paris," Vincent Van Gogh (1886)

Slow Dancing

*A poetic antidote to giving up our souls to Artificial Intelligence
Or Hal-the-computer on the dance floor to the sound track of* Blade Runner's *theme music by Evangelos Odysseas Papathanassiou*

Multi-layered confusion of pubescence:

Time and space,
So gently swaying in the back of a palatial Chevy.

Time and space,
Made of the velvety feel of cramped back seat flesh.

Feverish ebullition of teenage anticipation
Of darkened rural roads and noisy entrance
Onto over-heated dance floor and among over-heated bodies.

Furtive glances at budding curves,
Under flowered transparency of cotton and tempting guesses.

Strobe light illusive glances,
Revealing treasures of strangeness of that other sex.

Generous reciprocal synesthesia under colored lights,
Feeding eternal questions and envies.

Nature's ingredients of bodies meeting their destinies,
In this unpretentious caldron of cheap aluminum streamers.

Mumbled offer to dance.
Sweaty contact of left hand to sparrow-like trembling of hers.
Awkward embrace of right forearm passing over the protrusions of bra-hooks.

And first... Deep perception into her eyes,
Filled with mixture of inquiry and submission.

Resistance of muscular stiffness of her posture,
Followed by splendid abandonment of curving hips into his.

Evolution had done, that night, on that dance floor,
One of its un-programmed, swan-song best.

Reflection on the exponentially explosive increases in A.I. [artificial intelligence] making scientists speculate about the concept of the 'singularity' of machine-knowledge in the future. To paraphrase: Computers doing, feeling and or knowing the equivalent and more than what humans can with only our biologically based evolution.

Warm Sand

Daydreams
Of curly blond hair and long slender body
Of school's varsity second baseman.

Daydreams
Of father's aftershave in geometry class
Evaporating from troubling open-shirt.

Daydreams
Of junior prom in overheated gym:
First slow dance with first boy.

Followed by timid glances and awkward embrace,
Envious classmates and overjoyed girl-friend.

Seagulls calling for the sun to set.
Mother's inquisitive voice bringing back reality.

Left with sinking hands in the warm sand,
Burning cheeks and pink traces,

With budding thoughts of womanhood.

Going through box of photographs: Teenage girl sitting on the sand looking at sunset.

Verbal Architecture of Past Happiness

Love and hurt in the internet age

Once again,
Words of steamy circuitry under his amazed gaze.

Inenarrable things and feelings from the deep of sleepless nights:
Verb-less utterances, pregnant with explosive insinuations.

Breathless grammar and metaphors made of the richness of classical pearls:
Hedonistic beaches. Pre-Biblical happiness full of godless natural joys.

Frescos of personifications of unrestricted envies and carnal humidity.
Romantic abandonment on canvases full of the ghost of Delacroix:

With flesh upon flesh. Colors upon colors.
Crimson jewels sparkling among the fold of lazy bodies.

No longer dialogs full of cooling platitudes,
Emasculating monotonous frigidities.

Knowing references to international economics
And properly medicated non-sensual body parts.

Form and content,
That had been wrapped in perfectly constructed syntax:
Acting the part of plaster of Paris,
As a prudish white-wash over moribund realities.

A love letter... now, under his gaze:
Reconstructing in verbal abstractions

Love's minutiae coming suddenly back to life,
As he read the vapors of her end-of-day preparations:

Applying his favorite perfume to appropriate favorite areas,

For the wrong recipient.

Ex-lover receiving by mistake a steamy love note addressed to the new significant other.

Bluish marble

Wisps of prairie-green gentleness.
Streaks of bluish peace.

Precious solitary human presence
Recessed in a cocoon
Between limpid river flow and aromatic mountain pines.

All seems well… All feels well.
All is in its respectful place.

Majesty of orchestration
Playing to the accompanying nuptials
Of nature's generosity.

In awe of the impressively and statistically improbable beauty of nature during a rare nature walk.

Google Earth and Heartbreak

Another gadget. Another timid step…
Into this strange Brave New World made of silicon crystals

The new tea leaves, the new Prophets of destiny
In a new age of wisdom.

Speed of light imposing wild eyed surprises at key stroke speed.

We want to know because we can.
We want to see because we yearn.

We all want to turn around
To see Sodom and Gomorrah.

We turn over our inner whims and entrust them
To the vagaries of the inorganic guts of algorithmic programs.

We dare to pile, in a sadistic way, the harsh solidities of the present
Upon the fine dust of the past.

Scoffing at the deep seated voices of human wisdom
Warning us of our body's too easy craving of daily sweets of nourishment

While our soul, to survive, needs instead
Regiments of natural illusions and dreams.

But dare we must… and dare we do.
So we press … the enter key:

It then appears… in attractive simulated reality
This momentary facsimile of what things have become.

We recognize the dead frigidity of Time past
Under the abject confusion of the unrecognizable present
As mere footprints of cherished places
Erased by years and mankind.

Using Google Earth: The heartbreak upon looking at tree top level upon the unrecognizable and seemingly evaporated precious landscape of youth: "I would have been better off not knowing" he whispered.

The end of everything

From on high,
Echoes of pseudo-biblical admonitions:
Stern warnings with Old Testament undertones.

"You live by the Internet… You will die by it!"

Pie in the sky beliefs in Cloud Technology:
Concrete reliance on vaporous molecules
Whose collective dissolve would level knowledge,

Full of conflicted envy and disdain,
The Vandals still left us vestiges of Rome.
The black plague spared enough green sprouts
of human passion for continuation.

While stockpiled visual and literary treasures
Would dissipate down to their un-retrievably primordial binary elements
In an unprecedented solar flare moment.

Everything that is anything could go "away": Uploading some music and realizing that it will be in "the cloud". What will remain after a massive solar flare fries everything?

Total recall

Wizardry of blinking lights. Alchemy of futuristic potions.
Mind bending results.

Rows of bodies in the safety of plastic cocoons.
Dichotomy of hospital sterility and restraining corporal belts.

Various groans and explosive movements.
Squeals of delight and fear.

Beads of sweat and rising temperatures
Safely controlled and monitored.

Bank tellers and school teachers living up to and beyond
The gates of the gratuitous and the acceptable.

All of this Brave New World of knowing computer programs,
Satisfying the thirst of these sedate lives.

The whole surrealist scene conducted magistrally
Under the computer baton of the gifted supervisor:

In this, the hellish laboratory of the future minds answering future needs.

This same scientist surreptitiously going home at night,
Favorite wine in briefcase,

To inhale the uncorrupted and un-enhanced bodily smells of satiation,
 On the rough simplicity of cotton sheets,
In the arms of his partner.

Advances in scans and biological studies of the brain seem to indicate that our thoughts and memories can be reduced to chemical impulses which we perceive as reality. A line from one of the protagonist in *Total Recall* (2012) suggests that we could thus skip concrete, physical reality and fabricate it as it suits us. Here we have a scientist who works daily with this opiate of the future.

Sounds and Silence in the Kitchen

Awkward mindless re-adjustment of salt and pepper shakers…
Symbolic pawns of lost souls
On the flowered table cloth tapestry.

Twisted hand towel…
Languishly seeming to ooze childhood memories.

Merciful shadows from antiquated light fixtures
    Reciprocally hiding humid faces.

Clair-obscur reflections on parental glances
Speaking unspoken questions.

Noisy silence
Answered by the voices of tortured souls.

Immemorial human theatre
Of classical worries, reconstruction and reconciliation
Played between the sink and creaky cupboards.

Deep sighs of faithful half blind golden retriever
Keeping lids half opened to re-confirm this sudden appearance

Of the return of the son… the soldier…
Both now made prodigal against their will.

[David Grossman making reference to his book Au chevet d'Israël, Édition du Seuil]
"… Il y a une scène qui résume l'effet de la guerre sur les rapports familiaux. Ofer [le fils] revient en permission. Il a vu des brutalités, des horreurs, les affrontements avec les Palestiniens, les colons. Il ouvre la porte, je me souviens de ce premier regard sur la maison, j'ai moi-même été soldat, il ne croit plus que tant de tendresse existe. Vous devez vous réhabituer à votre mère, votre famille, votre lit, vos livres… Vous devenez de plus en plus dur. Je crois que les moments les plus importants de l'histoire se produisent aussi dans les cuisines, les chambres à coucher, et pas uniquement sur les champs de bataille. »

"There is a scene that resumes the effect of war on family relationships. Ofer [the son] returns home on leave. He has seen brutalities, horrors, confrontations with settlers. He

opens the door... I remember this first glance on the house, I... myself was a soldier... he can no longer believe that so much love can exist. You have to get used to your mother again, your family, your bed, your books... You progressively harden yourself. I believe the most important moments of history take place also in kitchens, bedrooms, and not only on the battle fields."

Source : Paris-Match 3253. September 2011. Interview by Aurélie Raya of David Grossman p.35.

Monet's depiction of the joys of living. (La Grenouillére (1869))

Denied

Favorite one eyed-Teddy bear
Still on wobbly dresser

Twice a year, the sweep of the sun
Hits this precious corner of his room

A celestial calendar
Sole reminder of the slide of Time

Yellowing newspaper pictures
Full of the solemnity of military and civic honors

Strange tenderness of makeshift altar to teenage years
Frozen by parental tears

All forward movement stopped
By a quasi-spiritual act of solidarity

For fellow comrades in inexplicable irrationality
That would eternally deny him the intimacies of human happiness

Thoughts about what a young casualty of war will never know after jumping on a grenade to save his comrades.

Inconvenient

Swirls of unbridled violence done to body parts
Still floating in hallucinating brain.

Winds of things done and seen
Done and done for alleged uncompromising ideals.

Creaky joints of fragile tendons
Joining those of rusty shopping carts.

Eternal wounds of the mind and heart
Bought at the indecent shameful price by sparkling medals.

Guttural mortal cries of comrades
Still echoing against lonely street signs.

He conveniently lives where old soldiers have too often lived…
… In the unclean shadows of daily lives…

… The embodiment of inconvenient fetid refuse of yesterday's callous actions

Invading… if we dare allow it,
The conscious… of the righteous.

Symbolic Viet Nam era veteran in an empty lot within sight of the Brooklyn Bridge.

Amplification

Daily rounds to appropriately sized tiny house:
Hallway photographs painful like the Stations of the Cross.

Neighborly check full of the balm of silence:
Ointment for myriad of ailments in left-over shell of war body.

Rock hard Korean-mud chiseled by truck tires,
Late cold of late winter of battle,
Ringing in ears still echoing with metal tank clanking,
Un-dying sharp knee pain from unlucky sharpshooter.

Nothing and no-one could any longer endanger his shacking sclerosis frame:
Life and history had done all they could.

Etching barbs of sleepless nights in the marble of his dying heart
In this… Marble of a man.

Hence the uncharacteristic tears in this man's washed out eyes:
"My dog died yesterday…" in wet syllables.

Had he found, in his favorite chair, an opportunity to cry openly,
Hiding the still raw loss of his wife… his army buddy… or his Golden Retriever?

To this day… It was not clear which of these deaths
Haunted him… Until his.

Reflection on visits with old veteran neighbor, witness to too much.

Replaced

Anonymously shielded by the vagaries of military roulette-wheel:
A blank face took his place.

Having dutifully taken his forward step upon the morning call,
Firmly answering to his last name, first name and number.

Smartly acknowledging his new assignment
And silently packing his socks.

His duffle bag and basic training in tow,
In a perverted religious ritual,

Christ-like figure without the wood and nails:
He took someone else's place,

Replacing only the body
Since it could not replace the soul.

Transferring the late night maternal anguish
To the altar of another mother's kitchen table.

Viet Nam ex-draftee who was "excused" from war as a result of a family tragedy who, years later, cannot balance the book of life and responsibility: "Someone had to have taken my place to fill the basic training platoon count" he whispered to himself: with whiskers of cheap beer and salty tears rolling down to his chin.

Patches of Meaning

Nobility in the inner simplicity of actions
Scattered in the debris on the waves of human agonies.

Things done with an aura of moral purity
With essences of natural moral authenticity
In otherwise silent universe.

Concentration camp prisoners reciting poetry to each other.
Lactating women giving the breast to war orphans.
Anonymous conscript sacrificing his valuable food.

Anecdotal examples of the average among us
Magnanimously shining in darkest tunnels..

The grand ball of life, living and dying
Would have gone on with or without their benevolent attendance:
For like the weather, these forces do not know their own cruelty

But it is in these minute, effacing gestures...
By the feathery gentleness of their impact...
Their unpretentious generosity...

That the righteous keep repelling death at the gates of life:
Thus redefining and reclaiming its dignity for the rest of us.

Reflecting about acts of pure human solidarity amidst human-made hell: With a thought toward Albert Camus.

Different Endings

Games. Expansion of youthful energy.
Friendly contests of boyhood dexterity and ability:
Malicious disobedience of throwing of stones and climbing of rocks.
Reciprocal taunting laughter and sly remarks.

Perched in centenarian olive trees.
Squeezing of Provencal bluish lavender tips,
To the perfumed release of innocent solar essences of an antediluvian universe.

Two young boys in the protective cocoon
Of nature's sane sequence of Things and People:
Pastoral goodness sprinkled with gems of prosaic happiness.

From the kitchen window: Late afternoon supper call,
Followed by infernal entrance through the gates of reality:

Intrusion of acrid acids in the milk of insouciance.

Leaving one with a plate of tepid watery soup and an infected memory.
The other... To an orphaned destiny...
Among the thorns of the Maquis.

Inspired by Un sac de billes [A Bag of Marbles] *by Joseph Joffo. An autobiographical novel about Joffo's survival as a Jewish young man during the German occupation of France.*

And,

Members of author family's recollections** from one of two boys who had been playing in the hills of Provence during World War Two: a normal event for children but for the presence of wartime. Unbeknownst to one, his new playmate had just been made an orphan. Upon leaving, the stranger hinted that he had no parents to whom to return. They would never see each other again.
** With some narrative liberties for literary flexibility.

_You should go home.
_ I can't ... My parents are dead.

Priorities

Displayed noodle soup results
Of computer generated MapQuest road directions
From the bowels of insensitive programs.

Last minute cellular calls
For last minute attention to urgent minutia.

Imperfect weather forecast
Forecasting unsightly dripping hair and wet socks.

Perceived or assumed social slights,
Sprinkled with religious overtones of Holiday table remarks,
To quiet the conscience troubled by a resurging unconscious.

Illusionary and delusionary plans
That would have made up for lost time at a later time.

Macabre humor from jaded humor
To insulate us from anguish about our own pointless existence.

Critical mass of emotions and images
In explosive visions over the empty funeral parking lot landscape.

Reconstructing details of the departed's life,
By forming an avatar of his presence...
To appease his guilt.

Inspired by the Memorial of a loved one and reflecting about having let scheduling choices prevent what would have been a last visit before his death.

I.C.U.

Circular setting of death and dying.
Architectural roulette-wheel spreading the chances of happy endings.

Labored aspiration and quicker expiration.
Clammy hands clutching at pale sheets.
Burning eyes blindly hoping for familiar silhouettes.

Shooting pains and missing limbs:
Spousal abuse or poetic justice for drunken spree.

Crazed zigzagging screens displaying chilling numbers.
While beeping alarms echo sleepless nights.

Uncontrolled bodily functions and tangled plastic tubing:
Returning dignity to early childhood dependability.

Somber corner conversations about lasting momentous decisions:
Akin to red-clothed Cardinals ushering dying papal hours.

Restricted club membership of the damned,
This infernal merry-go-round,
But without the soothing gentleness of a Beatrice.

Tear filled humid phone calls answered by strict rules and professional restraint:
Distancing the dangers of familiarity, intimacy and personal feelings.

Fine line in this circular world between frigid tones
And proper respect for cooling withering life.

And amidst all of this misery and pain:
This dead-end of people and things,

These moist multicolored cupcakes appear… Shyly…
On the metal of the corner of a night shift schedule table.

Sterility and human agony could not… Would not dare contradict
What at time… Pieces of life do best… In the most concrete way,

That is…
To gently push aside, thanks to these multi-colored symbols
And to glorify in this waste land… A beating new life.

Intensive care unit staff reacting to one of them bringing cupcakes celebrating a colleague's upcoming maternity leave.

Note: hospitals put the patients' rooms around the I.C.U. medical staff station.

Gods and Codes

Crystalline world of Mediterranean beginnings.
Great gods on alkaline Grecian hilltops in bleached landscapes.

Marble gazes from powerful names
Of apparently powerful Mythological tells

Wisps of burnt incense from Holy of Holies
Interlaced with electric sounds of translucent sheers upon sensual sheers
Sinuously hugging Temple maidens in the carnal breeze.

Food for very human thought, sight and senses:
Mixing the geometric and sensual
To the needs for intellectual and public order

New home for these massive egos
In the massive echoes among Gothic arches.

Submissive masses passing under portico of hauts-reliefs.
Crescent scenes of Hellish proximity and elusive Paradise.

These gods are not dead:
We still live under their omniscient glance

And under their assumed and accepted forms
As lines of computer codes.

Fantasy of seeing the omniscient gods of the classical Mediterranean world finding their way to the automated, directional guidance controls of modern airliners under the guise of binary lines of computer codes.

Yellow Light

Hellish domestic disturbance:
Endgame play taking place on stage of food strewn greenish linoleum,
In this, a Commedia dell'arte with well-established actors.

The drunken and feverishly crazed husband.
Properly beaten wife in the corner by the stove.

And the extras... The peripheral casualties for this setting of urban misery:
The two children huddled in their bedrooms
With their ineffectual Teddy bears.

An ideal sociologist's Petri dish,
Containing the freshly picked neighborhood ingredients,

Of missing parts of things, people and life:
That could make for humans... living humanely.

Proper promiscuous space for this microcosm of pain.
Wasted words of last minute dime-store wisdom
About throwing life away and loved progeny.

Fog of war inattention to police protocol,
Mangled by confused disorientation.

The yelling... The pleading,
The yelling... The pleading.

Hitchcock speed of slashing images of details seen and unseen:

Ice pick hidden in coat pocket
And mind set to correct all the flaws of life...
All the real or perceived inequities,

In one last quick plunge.

And a middle age sergeant...
On the floor and lifelong brain damage.

Wallpaper scenes going through his mind,
As he moderates his indignation for a traffic ticket.

Fuming with anger for a moving violation: going through a 'late' yellow light at one in the morning.

Past Third and Going Home

Rich diversity of girls from resulting American melting pot.
Multi language row of apartments linked to nuances of shades of hair.

The boys had no thoughts of war,
Giving furtive looks towards the stands,
Returning glances from Polish and Italian female admirers.

Pete had hit a triple and "Sure-Swing" Richard was their best hope.
Sweaty athletic beginnings from teenagers into men
Under a late New England summer sun.

Taunts from the guys from other street
Drowned by their neighborhood friends.

He was up… It felt good to have this next moment well in hand:
A kind offering from sport divinities of some sort of earthly happiness.

A swing of the bat into proverbial victory lap:
The game was won and life remained good.

Richard did not bother to stay at home plate.
He didn't bask in glory.
He knew he was and had been late for supper.

Down the hill toward the Thames,
Up Bank Street and envious glances of cool breezes off Fisher's Island,
Around the Italian stores and his father's fishing spot.

Up the wooden steps and the creaky patio:
Reputed haunt of a young Eugene O'Neil.

Vague sounds of women's voices,
Low drone of uncharacteristic household peace
Matching the dignity of the rich dark-veined paneling:
Giving the main living room the aura of churchly whispers.

No chastising call for clean hands.

No mention of "cold dinner for you young man!"

No reference to lack of equal scholarly effort
To that of sport ambitions.

Instead, a bottomless sadness in watery eyes
And enigmatic rictus of pain on his mother's lips.

The game was over.
His team had won.

His father had died somewhere in the war.
Life and living were changed… forever.

Teenagers playing baseball during a New England Summer afternoon while WWII rages on, at the age when a home run could solve all your worries.

Custer's Last Stand

He already had his war paint applied by sunrise.
His bride had furtively admired his virile stature while giving her breast to their child.

Acrid morning fires had been smoldered and horses fed.
Time had come to ride over to the Holy place and make a Holy stand.

He returned with only a flesh wound,
And the celebrating echoed to the vibrating deep-night stars:

They had saved the solidity of the Sacred
And their children would continue to gaze at the mist over the irreplaceable.

Violence had thus been done and would be done again...
... In the shadows of the Black Hills.

A peripheral issue, for the resettlement of the Indians tribes from the sacred site of the Black Hills, was the presence of gold, eyed by the United States Treasury.

Natural Laws and Gods

Solid directions from flimsy fumes of convictions
Unquestionably repeating previous beliefs living in the past
Where they had lived comfortably.

Wondering if these voices of canons of truths
Were induced by self-serving distortions in mirrors
or intolerant clarities of the soul

Sterility late in the night to look for absolutes
By red-clad arrogant Grand Inquisitors

God-speak-fragile divinities
Invented by mankind

With all the accompanying ignored frailties
Of their very own human makers

Along with very earthly consequences.

Upon reading another entry [New Scholarly Books section of Chronicle Review section B] of a newly published analysis of the sources of all societies' attempts to self-govern with laws [regarding happiness, ownership, privacy, personhood etc...] and the ultimate debate as to their ultimate origins, divine, natural, and what difference this could make in their ultimate inerrability.

Dreamscape

Akin to voyeuristic tourism
Into the innocence of shameless hedonism.

Solar intimacy of naked skin:
Dionysus at play in Saint-Tropez.

Unshackled from biblical edicts:
Citizens of a garden variety of heavenly gardens.

Guiltless. Clear conscience,
In spite of the splendid exposition
Of divine private attributes
Found between the Renaissance-like placed greenery
And generic genitalia.

Street-scape of happily nude shoppers.
Of attentive new mothers leaning toward their broods.
Officers of the law strapping their deadly gear over middle-age bulges.

Appropriately sun drenched and ventilated groins
Of all sorts and all ages.

A world where it had been dictated,
By earlier and therefore much wiser beings,
Rendered infallible by their status as Founding Fathers:

Having decreed long ago that such goings-on
Should be so,
Continue to be so,
And be protected.

All was well in this world of the vestmentary liberated

When he woke up:

In the alternate and too real world
Of other truths and other beliefs…

Of promoted and protected gun ownership.

Not unlike the unalienable right
Of buying your gallon of milk in the buff.

Channeling Voltaire and Jonathan Swift

A Good Start

To the overture music of A Space Odyssey

Jumble of fallen trees and confusion of guttural groans.
Broken branches and missing bloodied limbs.

The dying fire... Dying along its dying warmth.
Fearful glances into the hieroglyphics made by lightning strikes.

Huddled proto-beings under shapeless animal skins,
Looking haggardly into opaque skies.

Instinctive moves from reptilian side of brain,
Searching for self-preservation and the next minutes of life.

In this...
Another prehistoric, diluvian, one-sided event:

Pairing the youth of mankind
In its apparently pre-judgmental days...
... Against nature's mindless fury.

Not a hopeful scene... Until... Until...

The act by this hairy beast of a male,
Grabbing a crying baby from the mud.

Scientists believe that what might have evolved into the capacity for moral judgment in the modern brain could have its source in the survival of positive evolutionary genes: e.g. Tribes, where members helped each other, thrived.

Poem inspired by an address by the atheist Albert Camus in front of Dominican priests on the ability and source of the conceptualization of 'good' and 'evil' in a nihilistic universe: "I shall not, as far as I am concerned, try to pass myself off as a Christian in your presence. I share with you the same revulsion from evil. But I do not share your hope, and I continue to struggle against this universe in which children suffer and die." Albert Camus, in The Unbeliever and Christians, Resistance, Rebellion, and Death, *Edited by James A Haught.*

One Size Fits All

Contented high priests, on high bench, on high court
Full of their clarity
While gazing into fumes from scented temples altars,

Akin to village chieftains extracting meaning
Written in sinuous sanguine stains from chicken innards,

Akin to charlatans declaring divine translucence
In the opacity of coffee grounds.

Echoes of black magic from these black robes
Looking for signs, in wispy clouds,

Of Constitutional original intent.

Making attempts to read any linkage between the horse and buggy,
Satellite positioning technology
And the words on this crinkly document.

Stubbornly using an Eighteenth Century document to decipher how it would apply to daily modern life.

"In The Chronicle of the Constitutional Contradiction, for example, Crenshaw questioned framers of the Constitution and the compromises they made for slavery, thereby identifying the constitutional snake in the garden of 'originalism' (the commitment among conservative judges to interpreting the modern Constitution bases exclusively on what the founders thought). From The Chronicle Review *(October 21, 2011) Article by Lani Guiner and Gerald Torres on the passing of Derrick Bell. [Nota bene: the poem was written before the reading of this article]*

Ideals and Fairytales

Channeling Jonathan Swift

Not much idealism left unscathed
After studying between the lines and beyond the lines.

Childhood years in the warm porridge
Simmered in the mythology of history manuals:
Bland food ingested, beak to gullet, as predigested scholastic morsels.

Things and people: Seemingly of biblical drive and wisdom.
Tells of toppling cherry trees and no more lives to give.
Two if by sea and Manifest Destinies.

Innocence of Norman Rockwell purity of the Freedom of Speech
Soiled by the sewage of abuse and arrogance.

Crystalline succinctness of Declarations.
And amazing elasticity of Constitutions.

The will of the populace
Believed to be safe in its tabernacle
Of the precious and unquestioned.

How could these few well-meaning pages
Lead to anything but righteous endings?

———————————————————————

Mother Democracy looking suspiciously at her unrecognizable
syphilitic descendant:
The Filibuster and the Senatorial Hold.

The democratic principles soiled when a single Senator could stop the process such as in the early attempts at Civil Rights legislations.

Candide (Revisited)

Smells of success.
Doubly intoxicating beliefs in illusionary beliefs:
Convinced that the hirsute skins of our animal past
Have been neatly hung on the walls of our smoky caves.

Smugly civilized. Never to look back.
Powerful Voltairian garden full of metaphoric vegetables,
With aggressive weeds at its edge: Enviously trying to take over.

Omnipresent temptations... in the best of us,
To join the crowd... to search for gems on top of the heap.

We'll have to content ourselves
With less than a half measure of accomplishment.

We'll have to take, what we do, at the speed that we do it,
And like a dreamy Sisyphus, half way up his hill,
 Be glad that we are still capable to at least smell the acrid fumes of decomposition:

Hoping in an ever improving world,
For a floral hint of elusive perfume.

Reflection upon Doctor Pangloss' belief that the societies naturally evolve toward bettering themselves: "Everything is the best in the best of worlds."

In light of an article about the Jardim [garden] Gramacho dump in Rio De Janeiro. This mountain high dump has soiled this once pristine bay with foul runoff and thousands of human beings living on the pile of filth.

In light of Voltaire advocating that Candid cultivate his garden in a beautifully futile 'voltairian' effort against evil.

Also reference to the admonition by Voltaire at the conclusion of Candide *to 'cultivate our gardens:' Task seemingly meaningless and yet such a powerful promotion of life in contrast with the ills of the world.*

Pâté de campagne and Laissez-faire

Ironically feeling like a forced-fed goose:
With eyes bigger than stomach.
Intestinal grumbling protesting over-feeding.

The texture had been too temptalizing:

Proper balance of moisture and firmness.
Gentle presence of pistachio nuts and perfume of Armagnac.

All these ingredients conspiring to ignore common wisdom
Against overindulgence and proverbial free lunch.

Unfortunately highlighting once more the very human leaning
For transforming the individual good into a collective bad:

Reinforced by the breakfast media headlines.

Upon watching another analysis of the catastrophic Spanish real-estate collapse due to gargantuesque building frenzy. (The reader is free to substitute another personal choice of modern day economics)

Of Guano and Human Progress

Antithesis:
Heartbreaking irony of Pacific
As the baptismal name for this vast new expanse.

Darwinism:
Clash of sun-drenched indigenous skins
In awe of outer-worldly appearance of metallic invasions.

Arrogance:
Rapacious glance upon the tempting virginal landscapes,
In the perpendicular sight of wooden symbol of ancient punishment,
All soon to be pacified and properly Christianized.

Imposition of War of the Worlds true life ending
In this biological invasion imbedded in the coarse coats,
Wormy planks and bodily secretions of all kinds
That would tragically follow suit.

Not long after the heavy boot prints in the white sands had disappeared,
The acts and consequences to follow
Make the guano mounds appear, in the calculus of human behavior...

Pure and clean.

Inspired by Charles Mann's book 1493 in which "... [He] reveals how the voyages of Columbus reintroduced plants and animals that had been separated millions of years earlier, documenting how the ensuing exchange of flora and fauna between Eurasia and the Americas fostered a European rise."

The specific reference to 'guano' is related to the enormous Peruvian guano mounds that were mined for agricultural use by the Spaniards: the latters had to import to this "New World" Asian indentured, quasi-slave workers for the deadly, horrible backbreaking work.

The Pyramid Builder II

Stones set into the humid earth,
To make an un-godly mix of sweat and dirt:
Turning into a construct for the glue of misery.

Serpentine roads running into the belly of mountains.
Barren landscapes turned into horizontal transverses bending to the sky,
For the transcontinental fuming pleasure of a metallic snake.

Discounted exhaustion at the altar of mercantilism,
Paid at the un-holy exchange rate in broken bones, split skulls and hemorrhage of hope,
For all and any of these Pantheons of progress.

Muscular shoulders pounding the thin skin of this globe
Into proper visions of more riches.

Forgotten transparent glory of this anonymous worker
Simply claiming his seat at an evening meal table.

Homage to these anonymous workers who toiled on projects that shaped and reshaped our world and civilizations. Spurred by the viewing of an accounting in a documentary [The History Channel] about Boulder Dam[Hoover Dam] of the death of a man, apparently so disoriented by fatigue and fumes, that in a stupor he walked back to his job site and like an automaton started removing debris before the 'staggered blasting' was finished. Also, workers sickened by fumes were expeditiously taken out and quickly replaced for their lack of productivity. Apparently nothing had much changed since the building of the pyramids.
A first poem, entitled "The Pyramid Builder," appeared in Landscape of Evies[2010].

Pavlovian Sounds

Strange… the malleable distance between right and wrong:
That emotional space held together by insidious,
Snarly, disingenuous strings that bind us.

Circling around us into a convenient cocoon
Letting us claim imprisonment.

Strings and sounds invented for our collective consciences
And all around well-being.

And so… we have repeatedly left our crying wives and little children
At the cities' gates,
The railroad crossings and bus stations,
Disappearing foggy piers,
And dusty clouds on summer roads.

All that after being well rehearsed in the themes du jour:
Mine and not yours. This step and no more.
This hill and no other.
This weapon and its improvement.
Human and sub human. My God and this god.

On the way… drill sergeants and bolt clicking,
Slate washing of soul searching,
Brow beating and chest thumping,
And… the killing of the Other.

The whole thing well versed
In the absolution of chain of command culpability.

To the hymnal music of the tempting sirens of the sounds of war,
Taking us to that place where killing will be all right.

*"The alluring voices of the Sirens of Viet Nam
That would make killing all right."*

Unattributed statement by draftee (circa 1969) sitting on a foot locker in an Army post when the conversation had turned to "How can you teach someone to kill?

Abnormal in a Normal World

Infliction of sadistic treatment properly shared as proper family member:
Knowing personally both the sting and smells of burnt flesh.

Proverbially kicked as the lowest of the household in alcoholic ritual:
Big brown bedroom animal eyes as stand-in for the wife and children.

A Canine of God of sort…
Sacrificed symbol for all the societal ills of the workday.

Repressed animosity.
Un-verbalized mute hostility from behind dilapidated couch:
With just a hint of gleaming ivory rancor.

He had experienced nothing but the evil of man's hand on animal kind.

Finally and mercifully thrown out of the family's moving car:
Wet apparition at a retired couple's squeaky screen door:

And promptly biting the arthritic hand of the old lady:
For feeding him choice pieces of meat from their meager evening meal.

A dog, survivor of criminal abuse, dealing with the alien world of newfound kindness. The reader is free to substitute a child in second grade for the dog.

Of Instinctive Nurturing

Life born out of the hopeful maternal grimace
With anxious glances between her thighs.

Precious bleeding not wasted on secular violence
Giving continuing existence from constructive pain

Very human sculptural echoes
Of the similar submissive position from moments of procreation

Opening herself
Offering visceral gift from within

Characteristic primordial cry
Only joyous to maternal ears

First breath of child…End of labor
Beginning of giant cycle
Of loves, losses and tears

Making living
Too precious to be wasted on killing.

Heard in the iconic urban setting of a cultural party: "We would have been better off if women had run things."

Poem inspired by Désert from Le Clézio. After witnessing an unending cultural, tribal and political violence, Lalla the young shepherdess, comes back to her beloved North African desert to give birth to her daughter under the arid splendor of the Sahara sky. See index under Le Clézio for original French and then English translation for the powerful lyricism in the description of the scene.

Africa

To Lépold Sédar Senghor

On the slippery riverbank of Paleontological muds,
Running steps escaping deadly jaws.

Mother of us all…
Genesis of consciousness of the continuity of life,

You gently reclined among the trembling reeds,
Not far from the restlessness of the lustrous crocodiles,
And spreading you thighs, you somehow offered future days to our future.

Mother of us all…
Within nature's generosity, you gave us embryonic families,
Sending them on their march toward their goal…
In the hopeful mist of the next distant hills.

You labored to give us the placental tomorrows in the evolutionary chain…
Beginning whatever destiny we deserved.

By most accounts the African continent seems to be the main origin of modern mankind

Femme noire [Black Woman] by Léopold Senghor]

Nude woman, black woman,
Clothed in your color which is life, in your form which is beauty!
I have grown in your shadow while the sweetness of your hands cradled my eyes.
And high on the fiery pass, I find you, Earth's promise, in the heart of summer and the noon,
And your beauty blasts me full-heart like the flash of an eagle in the sun.

Nude mother, black mother,
Ripe fruit of firm flesh, deep rapture of dark wine, lips whose song is my song,
Savanna of pure horizons, savanna trembling at the East Wind's eager kisses,
Carved tom-tom, tight tom-tom, groaning under the hands of the conqueror,
Your heavy contralto is the spirit-song of the loved.

Nude mother, black mother,
Oil of no ripple or flow, calm oil on the flanks of the athlete, on the flanks of the princes of Mali,
Gazelle of heavenly binding, pearls are stars on the night of your skin;
Delights of the playful mind, the red sun's glint on your glistening skin
Under the shadow of your hair—my cares are brightened by the neighboring sun of your eyes.

Nude woman, black woman,
I sing your passing beauty, your form I fix in the Ageless Night
Before old jealous Destiny brings you down in the fire and gathers your ashes for the suckling life.

Compartmentalization

Evil walls of physical and moral rectitude.
Convenient spaces between the now…
And the rest of the rest of us.

Veils made of complex knots
To filter out pesky specks
Of conscience and doubt,

To better let justification slither through
To the other side of a cleared soul.

These men… who conceived of the unconceivable.
These men… who toiled on the monstrous realization of the nightmarish…
… Scenarios born in great minds… with little thoughts…

Went home at night to peacefully watch the Ed Sullivan show.

Reflecting on men who thought of, authorized, constructed and exploded the 'dirty plutonium bombs' of the Cold War.

Reparations: Camus and Capital Punishment

Crime and victim. Blood and flesh:
And their respective weight in the judicial scales.

Intent and depravity. Guilt and immorality.
Genocide of the bland generic
Versus the intimacy of the personal assault.

Between and among all these…
Vaporous concepts of re-equilibrium of these scales
Haunted by very tangible things.

Societies try to weave filigrees of reparations
Made of lines and paragraphs in codified forms,

Written in the cooler reflective emotions
Of cooler legal hallways.

The very words on the page taking the role of soothing balms and patches
Meant for direction… lessons… warning… and wisdom.

More hemorrhages… More blood-letting.
Instinctive stomach turning revulsion.

Instinctive… very human avoidance of the climactic ultimate payment
Appeasing society's good conscience,

Leaving us, however, to reflect upon the Angst
Of our own ultimate and unavoidable passage.

Reflection upon witnessing the frightened, incongruously human glance in the eyes of the genocidal criminal that was Moamar Kadhfy during his capture and imminent death caught on camera.

[Fragment of Albert Camus' paper on capital punishment where the author recalls a family member's physical reaction upon witnessing the application of the death penalty. The well-deserved instant of ultimate justice is overshadowed by the brutality of taking any life: no matter how worthless.]

... "One must believe that this ritual act [reference here to capital punishment] is quite horrible in order to be able to overwhelm the indignation of a simple and righteous man and the punishment that he felt was well deserved a hundred folds such that its main effect would be in the final analysis to cause him nausea. When supreme justice basically causes the honest man [whom she is purportedly protecting] to vomit, it seems difficult to maintain that it is indeed, as should be its function, the instrument of peace and order in the city. It is wildly evident that it is no less revulsive than the crime and that this new murder far from undoing the blow to society: instead adds a new stain to the first.
Arthur Koestler, Albert Camus. Réflexions sur la peine capitale, *Paris, Gallimard, Folio, 2002, p. 143-144.*

Obscenity

Real obscenity: this one non-verbalized.
Real obscenity: this one non-pictorial.
Real obscenity: this one self-indulgent and deadly selfish.

Intimate in a non-tactile... cold manner.
But nevertheless... Virile... Invasive... Repulsive.

Men in incestual relationships of the worst Biblical kind.
Men lusting after the goods and happiness of others.
Men coveting and playing with the life of his neighbor.

Shameless envy of temporal power in order to acquire
More... Of any kind... From any source.

Shameless false manipulation of gods, religions and temples:
For idol-worship of putrefied, deflowered values.

And surreptitiously convincing that 'citizen-other'
To follow, to love, to respect the whole insidious ugliness of the process:
Under the ribbon indecency of flags and honor.

That is obscenity.

Recognized as such when seen and heard,
In the whispers of the serpentine halls of the lobbies of politics:

To the background grunts and grind of mobilized soldiers of society
Vaporized under the muddy cruelty of the battle fields,

While dealmakers, arm dealers and facilitators sip their martinis:
Surrounded by the rich oak of historic establishments.

Leaders, with sweaty hands and backdoor winks:
Dealing their best deals... under the gaze of painted wigged predecessors.

Ironic that the newspaper columnists of Watergate fame, that illuminated the bankrupt philosophy and mindset of the Viet Nam war, used the iconic pornographic movie "Deep

Throat" as a reference for one of their sources.

With further reference to "Charlie's War" and "Casino Jack," when all sorts of hedonistic cavorting took place while weapons were sold as women and men died to defend so-called Democracy and American freedoms.

** Tangential reference to a Justice of the Supreme Court's comment that one should be able to personally define pornography when one sees it.

Temerity

The very banality of his spot on the calendar,
One among the other three hundred and sixty five of that year.

A date sorrowfully regressing in time,
Along with his thick black hair.

A date entered at various times in his life,
Under the heading of major steps in living:

Proudly given to grammar school teachers;
Solemnly attested to in front of local clergy;
Notarized among sheets of imposing mortgage papers.

Yet this date...
While hiding within an anonymous act
Of solely intimate significance,

... Had been a signpost... A reference to the instinctive need
For humans regaining human dignity:

A cry... Among the fighting and the killing...
As well as the first breaths of life,

... For a return to the biological order of things,
Within the still echoing sounds of despair, fear and hunger,

Precious and privileged moment at the end of nine months
In the hellish circles of mankind,
Impudently standing for the making of life...

... Among despair, fear and hunger.

Another Cognac fueled late night conversation topic: Could the children procreated in the last days of a war be interpreted as conceivable symbols of optimism?

Splendid Fragility

To Jorge Semprún

Splendid fragility of the cadence of words,
Holding back the mortal hammering of the cold.

Generous presence of the transparency of lyrical images
Caressing the discolored flesh.

Flowering metamorphosis of putrefied lesions
Given morning rose nuances. **

Filigree of intricate lace of fantastic allegories
Gently muffling in their rich earth the dying moans of bunkmate.

Magical alchemy of brittle wooden slats of barracks
Transformed into vaporous ribbons of Mediterranean clouds.

All of these repulsive smells and diseases
Kneeling for a moment of reconquered happiness
In front of such humanity.

Redemption from the sharp-edged hardness in this Dantesque universe,
Thanks to the whispers transmitted in this single act
In the midst of unspeakable horrors,

In the fashion La Pietà:
Cradled dignity of the last vestige
Of what is part of invincible human dignity…

Life.

** *Reference to a French Renaissance sonnet by Pierre de Ronsard*

In Literature or Life *by Jorge Semprún: [Semprún holding his dying comrade] … "I remember having already held the dying body of Maurice Halbwachs in my arms. It was the visceral shipwreck setting adrift a tearful soul that yet remained lucid until the last moments, a tiny, flickering flame no longer nourished by the body's vital oxygen."*

[Then Semprún recites these lines by Baudelaire]: « Ô mon vieux capitaine, il est temps, levons l'ancre… . » [Ah ! my old captain, it is time, raise the anchor… . » [Semprún's compagnion dies in an « pestilential explosion » of uncontrolled bodily functions.]

Literature or Life *[L'écriture ou la vie] by Jorge Semprún, Translated by Linda Coverdale, [Viking] Penguin Book USA 1997*

Number: 174517 **

Hellish centrifugal forces of the camps
Curving the linear tips of time
Thus making the past part of the future.

Thoughts of deep green varnish of olive tree leaves;
Lazy afternoon assembly of bottles of wine and crumbling goat cheese:
Rich varieties of ethnic ingredients under Mediterranean solar glory
In the sweet corners of youth.

Sounds from the gentle cocoon of familial laughter.
Layers of generations contemplating the past, the now and the future,
Played with the multiple chords of ordinary lives.

Then... the infection of the mind and body
From the malignancy of Auschwitz
And the acrid toxicity of mixing living-death with the living.

His body and soul had turned into a finished product,
Much before the bottom of the stair-case shaft.

A life with no more to add... Where too much had been subtracted.

The warped laws of physics and man
Had accomplished what science could only postulate:

The telescoping, as one...
Of the then... And the ever-after:
As a merciless frigid imposition upon reality.

Having walked away from his freedom,
With his first step into the Shoah,
 Did he regain it at the bottom of the elevator shaft?

With his past in frozen pieces still in his memory
And his destiny forever rewritten on the barrack walls of misery,

Did he ever reconcile living with a body freed...
Well before his mind?

** Primo Levy's concentration camp number

Inspired by the non-linear concept of time as exemplified in Slaughterhouse-Five *by Kurt Vonnegut: where the past, present and future exist as a completed whole. As a concentration camp prisoner, Primo Levy entered a world where his moments of teenage happiness would be forever integrated into a hopeless present.*

Beautiful ship

Oneness of drenched paternal mythology
Corporal vitality through virile strength
Sculptural definition made of sun-drenched crystals

Flesh made of happy youthful reflections
The whole apparently solid and unwavering

Absolute magical belief
Attached to the power of this sea creature

The Great Paternal… fashioned by the contours of youth
Filling the far corners of yesterday
With doubly humid images.

Easy illusions with magical powers
Nourishing Mediterranean paradise.

Day trip to the Pointe Rouge near Marseille when my father had put me on his back while swimming in the Mediterranean.

Le beau navire

Mythologie paternelle mouillée associée à celle marine.
Vigueur du corps à travers le viril musclé
Modelé de cristaux ensoleillés.

Chair aux reflets heureux de l'enfance
Le tout apparemment solide et inébranlable.

Féérie de la croyance absolue
À travers la force de ce corps marin.

Paternel… façonné selon les courbes de l'enfance
Remplissant les recoins d'hier
D'images doublement humides.

Illusions faciles, au pouvoir magique,
Nourrissant des bonheurs méditerranéens.

Un séjour à la Pointe Rouge à Marseille quand mon père m'avait mis sur son dos en nageant dans la Méditerranée.

The Ice Cream Truck

Fading bluish letters on the truck:
Like old tattoos on the soul.

Multicolored flavored memories
Of genesis of temptations.

Yet...
Annoying incongruity of uncontrollable sadness
Emanating from pipe organ rendition of this childhood tune.

If only...
It were possible to run once more down the street
To catch up with things virginal of flaws
And pregnant with idealism:

That afternoon in youth and summer,
That afternoon in youth and summer.

Memories stirred up by the simple innocence of the pipe organ music of an ice-cream truck.

Avatar

Still… that omnipresent sheen of style and posture
Both still splendidly present.

Dignified stern gentleness
Worthy of maternal warmth
Still floating in embers of past sensualities.

All the subtleties, all the motions,
All the tempting details
Present within arm's reach

All the satisfaction, frustration, confusion
Of an encounter with an avatar of things past.

Remnants in this still precious flesh
Recognized by a knowing flesh.

All still there
But only as vexing visions of an inorganic future.

Last scenes of movies such as Splendor in the Grass *or* The Way We Were, *where the lovers deal with the carnal remains of what once was.*

Digitized Debris

Where do old electronic love letters go to die?

They used to be members of the nobility of old feelings:
The caretakers of past moments.

These aristocratic descendants of torn and re-taped love letters:
Retrieved pieces from the paper basket;

Folded, un-creased and gently put to sleep
As mementos flattening themselves along with the passion
In a favorite English poetry anthology.

Or they would continue to exist...
Still in the oak tree trunk, in back of the garage:

These precious letters, all six of them,
First, middle and last initials
Losing their relief with each springs
To the re-awakening of the bark

Still continuing to silently express their meaning
In curves and straight lines.

———————————————————

Where... indeed,
Is the cemetery where old digitized words go to die?

How an unused, private email account known only to two persons becomes inactive and dies in the bowels of an internet server.

Love molecule

Needs and events sprinkled in the landscape of the mundane,
Satisfied by the habit of the moment.

Shirts with his favorite buttoned collars proudly hanging on the left side of polished cherry wood closets.

Rare guitar riff from an obscure band religiously played for adoring audiophile guests.

Vacations coming and ending with the proper appearance of solar happiness.

Tipsy late night accolades with colleagues, on occasions of all sorts,
In the vagueness of forgetful dialogues.

His mind had found blissful acceptance with the person facing him
Both in the morning mirror and in his arms:

Defining himself by seemingly remembering enough of his past,
While setting enough goals to satisfy his existentialist fibers.

The regularity of things and people matched by his obedience to the trivial,
Hiding under the cloak of trompe l'oeil happiness.

Acquisition of trinkets playing the role of opiate potions,
To dull any recurring sensation of the fear of repetition.

The presence or absence of any and all of these,
Adding to the calculus of futility.

All was well… that was going to end well.

Although… once in while… a quasi-religious rebirth would occur in his atheistic soul:

Probably preceded by the aftertaste of her favorite wine,

The particular virile laughter of an office colleague,

The flow of sound from street traffic filtering to him in a random bedroom
Through the lubricity of evening curtains,

Observing an anonymous woman's slim fingers on the safety railing of the commuter car,

The celestial copy of Monet's touch over a New England beach,

Or at the sight of the gentle wrinkles, between the index and the thumb, of the female companion of a woman's naked nape in a theater line.

And so naturally… so generously…from souvenir laden molecules,
Plaques made of instants… detached themselves.

Involuntary firings between dormant synapses reconstructed:
Essences… visions… and touch,

In swooning waves of uncontrollable memories.

How does the brain store sights, sounds, smells and touch and emotional feelings: in other words the very stuff that makes up art and gives some measure of meaning to our lives? Comment on Eric Kandel's The Age of Insight: The Quest to Understand the Unconscious in Art, Mind and the Brain."

A book where the Nobel Prize winner postulates that the presence of some sort of change in the molecular structure of the brain thus allows memory to continue: A sort of chemical memory making it possible to remember our emotions. A 'love molecule' for instance. It's ironic that such feelings would come from a mere molecule as illustrated below.

Loved Trait

To Charles Baudelaire and Alfred de Musset

Carnal fragrance vaporized into eternal seconds
Among quivers of limitless intimacy.

Roundness of the iris reflecting toward the lover
His image drowning in a loving glance.

Limitless seconds on the roundness of the iris
To the silent blinking of adored lashes.

Beaming sigh in the purity of an instant unveiling to the lover
The too timid sign so loved by a searching heart.

The distinctive trait in a lover.

Indice aimé

Hommage à Charles Baudelaire et Alfred de Musset

Fragrance charnelle volatilisée en secondes éternelles
Dans les frémissements d'une intimité sans limite.

Rondeur de l'iris qui reflète vers l'amant
Son image noyée dans l'amour du regard.

Secondes qui s'éternisent sur la rondeur de l'iris
Au battement silencieux de cils adorés.

Souffle épanoui d'un instant pur dévoilant à l'amant
L'indice aimé si timide servant de repère tant chéri.

Un trait distinctif chez la personne que l'on aime.

No longer of his world

Feats wrapped in capes of colorful daring.
Unbridled insolence signed with bloody swords
Sheathed in the warmth of honorable causes.

Friendships and enemies dealt with equal passion.
Riches made and gambled away in smoky soirées.

The mind and body can willfully
Live, die or survive in these pursuits of the mundane.

But at times,
The heart can come to know some higher truths
That forever place objects of ultimate desires
Next to other precious altar pieces:

In the fragility of a cocoon of their own vision of ethereal happiness.

No longer of his world,
Her sheen… now to be witnessed out of his embrace…

Both hearts forever made vulnerable by his imperfection.

Act II of Cyrano de Bergerac

ROXANNE : *His face shines with wit and intelligence. He's proud, noble, young, handsome….*
CYRANO: *Handsome!*
ROXANNE: *What is it? What's the matter?*
CYRANO: *Nothing… it's… it's only a twinge of pain from this little scratch.*

Considered like the turning point for Cyrano's resignation to the impossibility of any future with Roxanne.

Men and moths

Singed wings and crackling snaps of dying life.
Burnt essence of the powder of trembling visions of love.

Infernal fatal attraction of sinuous symbols.
Blinding white hot presence of emotional ethical blackness.

Reducing all values… all dimensions… all escapes
To one… and only one singularity of choice:

That of using the very last molecules of his soul
To declare his flame to hers.

Inspired by the folklore of fatal love tales such Don José's destructive affection for his Carmen in Bizet's opera. "Carmen… je t'aime" he cries, upon killing her.

There is a plant, common in South Africa, which can only reproduce itself when its seeds are made ready by prairie fires.

The Boxer and the Sparrow

Muscular arms shaped for the glare of media violence.
Bruised skin and bloodied features.
Grotesque puffy eyelids worthy of Quasimodo.

Brutish pas-de-deux in the burst of flash lights,
Twirling on enclosed canvas: glossy with bodily secretions.

This quasi primitive embodiment of contained rage,
Now captive in the overwhelming fragility of a woman's loving glance.

Visions of the Beauty and the Beast:
Now dancing all around the nuptial shadows on the wall.

___

Our universe was still left the better for it,
Despite their shortened happiness.

Fate is, after all, not so unfeeling:
Having proven her tender indulgence...

By allowing such romantic earthly moments
To be tasted by these two deserving souls.

Inspired by Marcel Cerdan and Édith Piaf's reciprocal and touching love affair until the boxer's tragic death in an airplane crash.

Sightless Images

Lost… The immediacy of timelessness:
Those sparkles of intensity in the glance.

Lost… The privileges of uninhibited freedom:
His wanderings through the exotic labyrinths
of her rich soul.

Having done his best to prepare,
And now… Facing his loss with a quasi-religious belief
                      In his aptitude to recreate from cinders…

… Pyric fires made of sensual dreams.

True as those dreams were true
 He knew that the past was his…

… Art had taught him so.

From the molecules of those embraces…
 Essences of her touch…
He would bring her back.

 He knew… He knew
That she had been the earth to his Titan soul.

Having been left
With no eyes in front of her image
No ears next to her sighs
No words next to her lips…

… But for her immortal attraction for his heart.

Art, any form of art, as the precious refuge for the people and things of the past.

An Eternal Second

Cosmic singularity of her features.
Evaporated universal constants faced with this still unformed moment.

The one containing an incestuous and improbable temporal intimacy:
Holding within... both the smallest particles of the past... and those of the future.

This with no laws, no limit nor distance.

Flexible time in the manner of Dali... where six o'clock loses its straight edge
In order to better cling to the curves of the hour glass.

It is in this singular eternal moment
When the first traces of wrinkles disappear in front of the majesty of impossibilities.

Cherished and sought moment
That the artist experiences once more through the imposition of his youthful glance upon things.

This body, these features, these eyes... Once so solid in their immediacy
And yet reduced to just a vague presence, a glance, a sigh:
Having since become but a humid dying breath.

Impossibility to turn away his glance.
To see anything else but this sofa.
To touch other stable objects. Thus allowing his own recognition:

Giving a familiar reference point in order to find an anchor in this world.

Eternal second
From which he awakens only after the opaque torpor of years.

These moments exist... He had expected them...
He had been forewarned.

He had feverishly read and re-read about them under the chaste covers of the glossy pages of teenage books of his adolescence.

… He had even sworn to prepare against them.

But once the black star near the pupil,
It was already too late…

… He lowers his gaze… He lowers his lips,
And following these gestures, all the words, all the wisdom from all the texts,
All the public oaths and all the good intimate intentions,
All that is geometric, stable and linear,
All of that will disintegrate in morsels of reality in front of his eyes…

All the dimensions of all times,
All the rich possibilities of voyages* into the tropical gratuity,
Were now displayed
Both outside of Time… And in his arms.

This reminded him of the beautiful oily and sinuous curves
Of carnal nonchalance painted on mythological and untouchable cotton sheets in academic works.

It would only be much later on, while drinking his coffee whose vapor would die on the window frost,
That he became aware that the months and years, since this plunge into the interior of this beautiful black star,
Had been the result of this moment of joyful consent.

"I could have chosen to not look into her eyes"
He fearfully told himself.

Inspired by these iconic movies scenes of the "first kiss" that unwind the plot of the film: in particular the video clip of "Tous les visages de l'amour" by Charles Aznavour. Also, linking the first moments of love to the scientific concepts of the first moments of the cosmos where time, as we know it, did not yet exist.

* "I become intoxicated with the combined smells of tar, musk and coconut oil." Sensations of an artificial voyage: Taken from "La chevelure" by Baudelaire [Petits poèmes en prose].

Une seconde éternelle

Singularité cosmique de son visage.
Constantes universelles évaporées face à ce moment encore informe.

Celui qui contient une intimité temporelle incestueuse et improbable :
Contenant à la fois, les plus infimes particules du passé… et celles du futur.

Cela sans lois, sans limites ni distances.
Temps flexible à la Dali… où dix-huit heures perd sa rectiligne
pour mieux épouser la sinuosité du sablier.

C'est le moment singulièrement éternel
Où la naissance des rides se résorbe devant la majesté des impossibles.

Moment chéri et recherché
Que l'artiste édifie à travers son imposition du regard de son enfance
sur les choses.

Ce corps, ce visage, ces yeux… si solides dans l'immédiat
et pourtant réduits à une présence, un regard, un souffle
devenus râle humide.

Impossibilité de détourner les yeux.
De ne voir autre chose sur le sofa.

De reconnaitre d'autres objets lui permettant de se reconnaître.
De lui donner une référence familiale.
Pour mieux s'ancrer dans ce monde.

Éternelle seconde
D'où il ne se réveillera qu'après la torpeur opaque des années.

Ces instants existent… il s'en était doué… il en avait été prévenu.
Il les avait fiévreusement lus et relus sous les couvertures pudiques du
papier glacé des romans d'aventures de son adolescence.
…il s'était même juré de s'y préparer

Mais une fois l'étoile noire proche de la pupille,
Il était déjà trop tard.

Il baisse le regard… Il baisse les lèvres,
Et à la suite de ces gestes, tous les mots, toutes les sagesses de tous les textes,

Tous les serments publics et toutes les bonnes intentions intimes,
Tout ce qui est géométrique, stable et linéaire,

Tout cela se désintègre en miettes de réalité devant ses yeux.
Toutes les dimensions de tous les temps,
Toutes les riches possibilités des voyages dans la gratuité tropicale,
Se trouvent maintenant disposées,
À la fois, hors du temps… et dans ses bras.

Cela lui rappelle les belles courbes huileuses et sinueuses
De la paresse charnelle peinte sur les draps mythologiques et intouchables
des tableaux académiques.

Ce ne fut que beaucoup plus tard, en buvant son café
dont la vapeur venait mourir sur le givre d'une fenêtre,

Qu'il se rendit compte que les mois et les années, depuis ce plongeon
à l'intérieur de cette belle étoile noire,
Avaient dépendu de son joyeux consentement :

« J'aurais pu, tout aussi bien ne pas choisir de la regarder dans les yeux »
Se dit-il avec frayeur.

Inspiré par ces scènes cinématographiques iconiques du premier baiser qui engendre l'histoire d'un film : Et en particulier le clip-vidéo de Charles Aznavour dans Tous les visages de l'amour.

Utilisant les concepts des premiers moments du cosmos comme métaphore des premiers moments de l'amour.

*« Je m'enivre des odeurs combinées du goudron, du musc et de l'huile de coco. » [I am drunk with the combined smells of tar, musk and coconut oil.]
La chevelure, Baudelaire « Petits poèmes en prose

Not Forgotten

Seismic aftershocks
Of surprising gentleness and source.

Long ago feelings of put away thoughts
Somehow still linked to the materiality of today.

Discovery of the singular solidity of the foundation
Between the duality of Things.

Love has never acknowledged fatal cracks in Time
Living, as it has always lived, in the fullness of all potentials.

Gothic transmission of emotions into a Merlin present:
Making anything appear as everything.

All it took was the slow, agonizingly slow movement
of continental masses of souvenirs,
Blindly scrapping against each other
Mounting each other in renewed abandonment.

Perfect storm of music and lyrics vibrating the soul:
Overtaking the coffee house, the chair, the table,
the hands and fingers holding the page,

Fusing everything with everything…
And everything with her.

Hearing "I Keep Forgettin'"… by Michael McDonald playing in a coffee house.

The name that must not be said

Once in one's life, a name develops to mean… Breathing:
Replacing the wind and the sun.

It sits us at supper tables
Overflowing with holiday plenty.

It sparkles on our morning curtains
Well before our nuptial awakenings.

Its very sound contains the fertile genesis of spring warming,
The magic comfort of a mother's voice.

We learn to let it envelop us:
Letting it enter our pores and molecules
With its sinuous syllables full of phonetic labial plasticity.

A magic name that the unknowing universe
Unknowingly offers to us:
As pieces of the mosaic that define and stabilize
our presence among things.

Once in a life time, our still pulsating soul, chisels that name,
Possessed and possessor, on the fabric of our being.

A name that we had won and have lost.
A name to never again gratuitously leave our unquenched lips.

A name… For fear of soiling its memory still full of a quasi-sanguine divinity,

A name… That shall suffer under our decree akin to an emotional
Pharaonic law:

Stating that it shall, henceforth not be heard… nor repeated,
Except as echoes in the chambers of the heart.

It shall be banned from the common spaces of the mundane
For the remaining moments of our existence.

Traditionally in Judaism, the name YE-HO-VAH is not pronounced but read during prayer as Adonai "my Lord" or HaShem "the Name." This was done due to its holiness and therefore out of reluctance to pronounce the name anywhere but in the Temple in Jerusalem.

Also, a reference to Moses, the Pharaoh's favorite falling out of favor and thus having his very name officially banned.

The reader is free to replace it with her or his own unmentionable personal name or point on the map erased due to geo-political decisions e.g. post World War Two.

The End of Simplicity

Unquestioned beliefs in the true heading of the Maternal Star.
Dependable appearance and re-appearance of Santa.

Benign cold of friendly snowflakes.
Visits from insightful tooth fairy among the gentle folds of morning cotton.

Feigned quiet anxiety of amorous destiny from daisy petals.
Summer vacations defined by the faithfulness of the sun.

Unfailing presence in garage corner of first bicycle.
Pliable warmth of grandma's chocolate cookies.
Vespers of quaint music of ice cream truck.

Calendars, friends, rituals... made sense,
By somehow knowing the role of their own innocence:

Until the ear-pounding, exhilarating, heart-crushing,
Bodily confusing glance from the girl at the next locker

And the crossing of the gates into post paradisiac complexity
Through this new landscape of impressionistic nuances of femininity.

Based on the scene in When Harry met Sally *with Billy Cristal regarding male versus female concept of friendship.*

Into dust

He saw the whole edifice… Precious and indestructible,
For what it was becoming:

Cards of memories, in a brutal game of Hearts
Collapsing unto itself into untidy layers in his soul.

There was something of the bedside mannerisms of a nurse in her demeanor:
Gentle but… aloof. Present… but elsewhere.
Attentive but… distracted. Here… but temporarily.

The rich, deep…
Seemingly bottomless sweetness of old conversations was gone:
Drained of the next instant. Void of pregnant silences.

Moments rendered sterile of their proper role
As precursors for multi layered banter.

Moments between the accidental touch of the hands
And the expected embrace.

The childlike excitement of putting off looking into her eyes:
To later confirm her perfumed glance upon him.

All of these dusty elements of a past universe
Were disintegrating in front of his consciousness of Things.

The world of the alchemic magic of Merlin:
The unrestrained passion of Tristan and Isolt,
… All gone

Things were reverting to the cold predictable repetition
Of the Table of the Elements.

No longer the wealth of surprises…
Rather the brute Newtonian logic of spinning and wayward dead stones.

Gone…
The multiple realities of the Human Element.

The unaccountability of the gratuitous,

And the awareness... The awareness ...
The grandiose and generous awareness...

Of living in these moments:
With no need for the smart circuitry of programs. No intermediaries.

Just the quasi-religious ... insatiable need
For a profane, hedonistic eternity.

All of these yearnings... all the richness of the instinctive... the visceral:
Diluted to watery warmth:

When he detected a new presence in her look...
... A certain indulgence.

Reflection on the wealth of scenes, from literature or movies, such as Les liaisons dangereuses *or* L'Arnaqueur [The Heartbreaker], *where lovers try to decipher each other's hidden emotional intent.*

"He detected charitable indulgence as the reason for her visit." Unattributed

En poussière

Il regarda l'édifice entier… Précieux et indestructible…
Se métamorphoser devant ses yeux :

Un château de cartes-souvenirs… D'un jeu de l'amour.

Le tout…
S'écroulant en désordre dans son âme.

Elle se comportait en infirmière près d'un lit :
Douce, mais distante. Là, mais ailleurs.
Attentive, mais distraite. Ici, mais temporairement.

Les anciennes, riches et douces conversations
D'une profondeur apparemment sans limite…
Disparues,

Desséchées de leur prochain instant. Vidées de leurs féconds silences.

Des moments…
Maintenant blanchis de leur vrai rôle :
Celui de précurseurs des plaisanteries aux multiples et fragiles feuilletés.

Des moments entre le contact accidentel des mains
Et celui de l'enlacement revendiqué.

Joie enfantine… Celle de retarder leurs regards réciproques :
Pour plus tard confirmer le parfum du sien sur lui.

Tous ces éléments poussiéreux d'un précédent univers
En poudre dans sa prise de conscience des Choses.

Le monde de la magie alchimique de Merlin.
La passion effrénée de Tristan et Iseult.
Tout cela disparu.

Les choses retournant à la froideur prévisible et répétitive
De la Table des Éléments.

Plus jamais cette richesse des surprises.
Maintenant,
 La logique brutale Newtonienne des cailloux morts tournoyants.

Perdues...
Les multiples réalités de l'élément humain :
L'imprévisible du moment gratuit.

Et la conscience... La conscience.
L'énorme et généreuse conscience.

Celle de vivre dans des instants
Hors des restreintes intelligentes des circuits programmés.
Sans aucuns intermédiaires.

Une simple insatiable soif quasi-religieuse
D'une éternité profane hédoniste.

Toutes ces envies...
Toute la richesse de l'instinctif... Du viscéral...
Diluées dans un bain attiédi,

Quand il détecta une nouvelle présence dans son regard :

Une certaine indulgence.

Réflexions sur les nombreuses scènes littéraires et cinématographiques comme celles dans "Les liaisons dangereuses" or L'Arnaqueur où les personnages jouent avec les émotions humaines.

« *Il remarqua un ton de charité dans la raison-d' être de sa visite.* » *[Non-attitré]*

Parallels

He had wished for proof, as he had long suspected,
That Mythologies could at any moment invade the world of Mortals.

That doors could open and introduce him to multiple possibilities.
That illusions and dreams were not all fabrications of disillusioned artists.

That the Big Bang drone of Faustian temptations
Could still be heard among the common filth of stacks of invoices
and Calvinistic duties.

That the beauty of the Devil was indeed
That He is still… beautiful:

And his embrace…
Doubly worth the eternal price he had always demanded.

That the beauty of dreams and envies can easily… too easily,
Impregnate susceptible ethics:

For like a Rembrandt's Bathsheba
His gaze was the gate to wilting moral ambivalence.

Such were his thoughts upon glancing over his right shoulder.
Upon a spell binding richness of intonations.

A multiplicity of incarnations and reincarnations of symbols:
Intelligence… femininity… strength and fragility,
Glancing all at once upon him.

The guilt of this moment would henceforth insist upon living on its selfish own:
Demanding its share of a parallel world.

A space filled with private memories and the scent of intimate happiness:
In epic seas swept by larger evils.

Office romance versus September 11, 2001: Deconstructing this bureaucrat falling in love with a colleague's wife while the announcements of the attacks on the Twin Towers turn on. Thus the precious first instants of love incongruously linked forever with pure evil. Inspired by an article by Alan Wolf in an essay of The Chronicle Review (September 16, 2011) "Evil Doers and Us" about the problems in dealing, defining or controlling evil.

Lace

It had been such a long time... since they had seen each other.
Such a long time… that this complex synesthesia
Made from perfumes, solar skin smoothness,
Still warm sighs made of early morning sheets,
Eternally steamy couscous and the lazy rocking of taxis.

She was now a prisoner in a new temple
Built from the realities of new stones.

Recalcitrant vestal incarnated by the sound of a disincarnated voice
Whose echoes had become a doubly absent presence similar to the street noises:
Finding only cold, flat and disinterested resonance
On the windows of his bedroom.

Her absence had transformed the minutes, hours and days into a lace
Whose rich interlaced beauty was reinforced by the airy presence of the voids.

Good survivor, he had become used to living on this lace where empty spaces predominated.

He carefully started to obstruct the holes with pieces of memories to better fight the frigid future.

He had managed a measure of living with a smaller measure of happiness
And could find nothing better to say to her, that day when she called than…

"I am trying to fill my life with things that are not you."

Homage to Jacques Brel

La dentelle

Longtemps… qu'ils ne s'étaient revus.
Longtemps… depuis cette complexe synesthésie
Faite de parfums, de chair lisse solaire,
De murmures encore chauds des draps du matin,
De couscous éternellement fumant et du ballotement paresseux des taxis.

Elle était maintenant prisonnière d'un nouveau temple
construit de la réalité de nouvelles pierres.

Réticente vestale incarnée dans le son d'une voix désincarnée
Aux échos devenus présence doublement absente :
Comme les bruits de la rue
qui ne trouvaient dans les vitres de sa chambre à coucher
Qu'une résonnance froide, plate et désintéressée.

Son absence avait transformait les minutes, les heures et les jours en dentelle
dont la riche beauté entrelacée était renforcée par la présence astrale des vides.

Il s'était habitué, en bon survivant, à vivre sur cette dentelle
où le rien prédominait.

Il commença minutieusement à boucher les trous
avec les débris de souvenirs pour ainsi arrêter le refroidissement futur.

Il s'était fait un petit chez soi avec un plus petit bonheur
et ne trouva rien d'autre à lui dire, ce jour-là quand elle lui téléphona que,

« J'essaie de remplir ma vie de choses qui ne sont pas toi. »

`

Hommage à Jacques Brel

Shaping the Future

He had discovered in himself the talent to transform grammar
Into a sort of appetizing purée.

Quasi canonical transmutation of matter:
Grammatical difficulties offering themselves on the altar of humor
Gesticulations, anecdotes.

In his eyes, nothing seemed to resist it.
Using culture: he could not miss the target.

From the start, he had noticed the effect of knowledgeable repartees,
Of dialogues, of the feminine gentleness of labial endings:
In this world with sounds of Teutonic undertones.

Wide opened eyes facing the riches of museums.
Culinary foretastes of iconic neighborhood bistros scenes.

He had done this with a feigned nonchalance:
He knew very well the impact on this intelligent thirst
Wanting only much more.

It was much later, upon learning of the consequences of his presence in the embryonic molecules of adolescence,
That he experienced the depth of existentialist anguish that he should have known well before.

Here, a French teacher [or for that matter any educator] upon learning about the existentialist, life altering impact of his course on the lifestyle choices of a student.

Façonner le futur

Il s'était découvert le talent de transformer la grammaire
En une sorte de potée appétissante

Transmutation quasi canonique de la matière :
Les difficultés linguistiques s'offraient sur l'autel de son humour
De ses gesticulations, des anecdotes.

À ses yeux, rien ne semblait y résister.
Le coup de grâce ne manquait jamais sa cible avec la culture.

Il avait remarqué dès le début l'effet des répliques savantes
 Des dialogues, des douceurs labiales des terminaisons féminines :
Dans ce monde aux sonorités teutoniques encore sous-jacentes.

Des yeux grands ouverts face aux richesses des musées
Des avant-goûts culinaires, des scènes iconiques, des restos de quartiers.

Il avait fait cela avec une nonchalance feinte :
Il connaissait très bien l'impact qu'il avait sur cette soif intelligente
Qui ne demandait que plus encore.

Ce n'est que plus tard, en apprenant les conséquences de sa présence
dans les molécules souches de l'adolescence
Qu'il ressenti les profondeurs de l'angoisse existentielle qu'il aurait dû
connaître bien avant.

Ici, un professeur [ou même n'importe quel enseignant] dans un lycée anglophone en apprenant comment son cours de français avait changé les choix personnels dans la vie d'une étudiante.

Counter-currents

Exquisite intelligence of sarcastic retort to sly comment:
Parental pride in such splendid imitation as proof of admiration.

Ease of words in flowing conversation
On varied topics: academic and scatological.

Authenticity of opinions that celebrate respect
For the dual status of an offspring in full self-assertion.

Repeated reference to respective personal quirks and general obsessions:
Well documented incapacity with any sort of tools
And infamously innovative use of plastic wrap and masking tape,

Followed by warm memories of insane mountain roads,
Incredible meals and Romanesque rural churches,

Obedient sunflower fields and bouts of Mistral,
Excursions into stone medieval streets and larger-than-life boulevards,

Chaotic trips to emergencies and rough pavement of early teen dates,
Emerging personalities and redefining boundaries:

The whole resulting in a nod of satisfaction
For having done the best possible in an unsatisfyingly
Imperfect world.

Strange conflicted projections into the future of our own, long lasting love and longing, for our parents and their rich memories in our hearts; and then, the longing images of us that we will have created, in turn, in the hearts of our own children.

The Effect of a Butterfly

Incongruous warmth on his nape... In ice storm.
 Familiar complexity of gentle floral perfume in bland office setting.
Similarity of sleepy femininity in remark from breakfast waitress.

Richness of overlaps in jaded present and hovering past,
Filtering through the murmuring lace of envies.

Moments between Parisian boulevards
And crescent-shaped New England beaches.

Nuptial sighs
Found between the Chiaroscuro of cicadas-fed white heat of Provence
And the frozen breaths of northern crystal nights.

Magic powers poetically emanating from its winged fragility:
Leaving him wallowing in front of a cooling cup of coffee
In order to extend the recurring illusions of a ghostly apparition.

A prophet of his own sorrow,
He had known his lot, well ahead of its time:

Appreciative of his privilege...
Dutifully recorded on the walls of his days
Since she had entered his soul in fluttering genesis,

Leaving him in the wake of her zigzagging beauty
As one of The Happy Few.

From the Canon of common wisdom: "We should be grateful to have known real happiness: even if short and only once."
Reflection also on the film: The Bridges of Madison County

L'effet d'un papillon

Tiédeur incongrue sur la nuque... Sous une pluie gelée.
Familiarité de ce parfum à la douce complexité florale, parmi la morne ambiance d'un bureau.
Similarité de la féminité mi-éveillée dans la remarque de la serveuse au petit déjeuner.

Amalgames d'un présent absent et d'un passé immédiat :
Le tout s'infiltrant à travers le tremblement de la dentelle de l'envie.

Des moments existant entre des boulevards parisiens
Et cette plage en forme de croissant du Labrador

Soupirs nuptiaux
Trouvés entre le clair-obscur de la chaleur stridente nourrie de cigales de Provence
Et ceux de l'intimité de soupirs glacés des nuits cristallines de la Nouvelle Angleterre.

Puissance magique construite de fragilité lyrique ailée :
Celle qui mène au regard éperdu devant le froid d'une tasse de café,
Tout en espérant retrouver l'illusion récurrente d'une apparition fantasmagorique aimée.

Prophète de sa propre douleur,
Il connaissait son sort, bien avant son heure:

Conscient de son privilège
Qu'il avait fidèlement transcrit sur les murs de ses jours,
Depuis la Genèse, dans son âme, d'un battement d'aile à la beauté zigzagante
Qui le laissa tout seul... Membre des Happy Few.

Inspiré du Canon de sagesse de tous les jours: « On doit être reconnaissant d'avoir connu le vrai bonheur: même si cela n'est que temporaire ou qu'une fois dans la vie."
Réflexion sur le film: The Bridges of Madison County.

Immortal Embers

Under the portal of the ever-present past.

Unlike the oscillations of well-behaved photons,
Unlike predictable bundles of energy,
Predictably dissipating their essences
In an increasingly darkening stellar void,

These embers had escaped...

Thanks to the mere arrogance made of their mere passion...

The powerful cosmological Einsteinian formulae
Meant to bend the universe to our cold intellect.

Time and space would have to be the landscape
Of things done, loved and gone:

So it had been written and so it would have to be.

The galaxies and constellations,
The exploding worlds and bright white pulsars:
All would come and go their own way.

Only to be remembered... in spite of their respective impact,
By the unstoppable weakening of their remaining dying beats
On the waves of black matter mud.

So it had been written and so it would be and have been.

But... In an obscure corner of things and people,
In an apparently forgotten speck of a moment:

Lost in the eyes of eternity,
Lost in time and space
Lost in the Now and Then...

All the rules of learned calculations,
All the dictates of what is possible,

All the extra heartbeats on Parisian bridges,
All the wet kisses under glass-domed train stations,
All the seemingly buried instants of aimless walks,
All the richness of intelligent banter:

All of it came back in a passionate reincarnation,
Akin to God's iconic Sistine gesture,
When... As he climbed on the moving train,

She folded the flesh of his index as it slipped out of her grasp.

The life of a bubble

For Noëlle and Luc

Bothersome echoes,
Of the formulas for the surface tension of liquids,

Found in the early hours
Of morning physics classes:

Intruding in this self-sustaining moment
Of the magic of youth.

No need for the artifice of complexity.
No need for the intelligent circuitries of digitized programs.

Just the simple spherical microcosm
Of solar reflections,

And the gentle presence
Of a visiting wind,

On this haphazard trajectory
Of happiness.

Watching the reciprocal happiness of children chasing bubbles in the summer sun.

EPILOGUE

Pierre Auguste Renoir immortalizing human intimacy.
(*Danse à Bougival*, 1883)

Light and Flesh

To the eternal Muse

Sulfurous clouds from the fissures of Hades.

Intoxicating Faustian images of eternal youth,
Telescoping years and decades
Into constricted swallows of sensual memories.

Pinkish folds under reddish waves of down intimacy.
Soft contours made for brushing kisses
Revived by his penetrating gaze,

Upon what,
From a cold and inanimate universe
Is truly a miraculous construct:

The singularity between
Ethereal photons of light and the corporal scent
Of his impression of reality.

« Sa peau repoussait encore moins la lumière que celle de tous les modèles que Renoir avait eus dans sa vie. »

"Her skin would reflect light even less than all other models that Renoir had had in his life."

From the book by Jean Renoir (Pierre-Auguste Renoir, Gallimard, 1981) describing Andrée, his father's alluring and young last model (Painting on adjacent page).

Glossary

A

A.O.C: Appellation d'origine contrôlée : French terminology for the names given to higher quality wines.

Anjou: Region on and around the Loire River south west of Paris. It gets its name from the city of Angers. Although the area is reputed for its white and rosé wines, it produces deliciously light reds.

Aznavour, Charles: French composer and singer, masterful at describing human emotions. Many of his works have become English language standards such as *Yesterday [Hier encore, j'avais vingt ans...]*.

Asymptote: Concept in calculus where the curve on a graph of an equation comes evermore close to a limit [a point or area on the graph] but never touches the latter. That subtle and subjective 'point' defended during my oral for my dissertation which, in my mind, is where the 'intent' and the treatment of syntax and the choice of vocabulary make the result 'poetic' for the reader.

B

Baudelaire, Charles: French poet whose poem "Correspondences" deals with overlapping relationships of senses such as colors and sounds, etc... . See Synesthesia.

Beatrice: The ideal woman who guides Dante through Paradise.

Bizet, Georges: Nineteenth Century French composer who captured the world of Provence in his *Suites*. In *Carmen*, he displays in memorable passages the misery of unreciprocated love.

Black Plague: Or the Bubonic Plague is estimated to have killed almost half of the population across Europe. Still, this calamity did not destroy Western civilization while a complete collapse of our digitized world could come closer.

Blanquette de veau: A light, velvety white sauce particularly suited for veal.

Brel, Jacques: Francophone singer from Belgium: Some of his songs are known in English and French for their heart-wrenching lyrics.

C

Camus, Albert: 1. French *'moralist'* philosopher and writer of a Universe with no divine absolutes. Known for his wartime courage in the Resistance and yet steadfast respect for life and mankind.

2. Original fragment of Camus' statement against capital punishment : "Il faut croire que cet acte rituel [la peine capitale] est bien horrible pour arriver à vaincre l'indignation d'un homme simple et droit et pour qu'un châtiment qu'il estimait cent fois mérité n'ait eu finalement d'autre effet que de lui retourner le cœur. Quand la suprême justice donne seulement à vomir à l'honnête homme qu'elle est censée protéger, il paraît difficile de soutenir qu'elle est destinée, comme ce devrait être sa fonction, à apporter plus de paix et d'ordre à la citée. Il éclate qu'elle n'est pas moins révoltante que le crime, et que ce nouveau meurtre, loin de réparer l'offense au corps social, ajoute une nouvelle souillure à la première." Arthur Koestler, Albert Camus. *Réflexions sur la peine capitale*, Paris, Gallimard, Folio, 2002, p. 143-144.

3. English language quote of Camus' speech to the Dominican priests from *The Unbeliever and Christians, Resistance, Rebellion, and Death*, p. 70, from James A Haught, ed, *2000 Years of Disbelief*.
French original "Je n'essaierai donc pas pour ma part de me faire chrétien devant vous. Je partage avec vous la même horreur du mal. Mais je ne partage pas votre espoir et je continue à lutter contre cet univers où des enfants souffrent et meurent." In *Fragments d'un exposé fait au couvent des dominicains de Latour-Maubourg en 1948* dans : Albert Camus, Actuelles. Chroniques (1944-1948), Paris, Gallimard, 1950.

Cinecittà: Italian for "Cinema City." Enormous film studio in Rome founded in 1937 by Benito Mussolini and part of the golden age of movie production later on during the 1960's and associated in later with Fellini.

Cosmic singularity: Scientific concept used by cosmologists to describe, among other things, the moment preceding the Big Bang or any comparable event when time does not exists as we know it.

Cyrano de Bergerac: Play by Edmond Rostand figuring a brave soldier who is very aware of how his large nose makes him repulsive to his love interest, Roxane.

D

Dali, Salvatore: Surrealist artist known for his 'melted' representations of solid object: Such as clocks.

Delacroix, Eugène: Nineteenth Century painter associated with the colorful Romantic school. In particular here, **Les femmes d'Alger dans leur appartement and Le massacre à Scio.**

E

Édith Piaf: Few moments of her apparent happiness, with the 'love of her life' Marcel Cerdan, came to a tragic end with his death in an air crash.

Elysian Fields: Meadows in Greek mythology where the favored of the gods would know only happiness.

Existentialism: Very generally, a philosophy of responsibility for one's actions, which, in their totality, define the individual.

F

Faust: German scholar dissatisfied with his life and willing to give his soul to the Devil for more knowledge and pleasures. Useful symbol as a literary portal to escapism and fantasy.

G

Godot: *Waiting for Godot*, Absurdist play by Samuel Becket whose characters aimlessly wait in vain for a person named Godot.

H

Hal: Malfunctioning computer on the space ship of the movie *Space Odyssey*. One of first better-known representation of Artificial Intelligence with 'self-awareness.'

Hitchcock, Alfred: Director of the movie *Psycho*: Referring to the rapidity of the shower scene where the mind reconstructs what is missed visually.

Hitchens, David: Iconic media personality and finely tuned thinker who made no secret of his continuing atheism in light of his impending death from cancer.

Hugo, Victor: Nineteenth century French poet and statesman. Some of his poetry made him recognized as a political leader.

L

Laissez-faire: From the French "leave it alone." Economic philosophy of "hands off" on the part of controls on individual decision making.

La Pietà: Iconic sculpture by Michelangelo of the Virgin Mary holding cradling her dead son.

Lamartine: Nineteenth century French Romantic poet and politician. He used some of his poetry for political purpose.

Le Clézio, Jean-Marie: French writer who captured the realities of colonial French presence in North Africa with historical precision and poetic imagery.

Le Clézio description of the birth : « La douleur à l'intérieur de son corps est maintenant comme une blessure, qui s'ouvre peu à peu et se déchire. Lalla ne peut plus penser à rien d'autre qu'à ce qu'elle voit, ce qu'elle entend, ce qu'elle sent. ... Le temps s'est ralenti à cause de la douleur, il bat au rythme des contractions de l'utérus. ... Instinctivement, elle retrouve les gestes ancestraux, les gestes dont la signification va au-delà d'elle-même, sans que personne n'ait eu à les lui apprendre. ... L'air entre enfin dans ses poumons, et au même instant, elle entend le cri aigu de l'enfant qui commence à pleurer. ... Puis elle s'allonge enfin au pied de l'arbre, la tête tout près du tronc si fort ; elle ouvre le manteau, elle prend le bébé dans ses bras et elle l'approche de ses seins gonflés... Elle regarde un instant la belle lumière du jour qui commence, et la mer si bleue, aux vagues obliques pareilles à des animaux qui courent.... Elle sent contre elle le petit être chaud qui se presse contre sa poitrine, qui veut vivre. » Gallimard 1980 (Collection Folio) pp.420-423

"The pain inside her body is now like a wound opening and ripping itself little by little. Lalla can think of nothing other than what she is seeing, what she is hearing, what she is feeling. ... Time has slowed down because of the pain; it beats to the rhythm of the contractions of her uterus. ... Instinctively she finds once more the ancestral gestures, the gestures whose meaning go beyond her, without anyone having had to teach them to her. ... The air finally enters in her lungs, and at the same time, she hears the high pitched sound of the child beginning to cry. ... She then lays at the foot of the tree, her head against the mighty trunk: She opens her coat; she takes the baby in her arms and brings it to her swollen breasts. ... She looks momentarily at the beautiful early morning light and the so beautiful blue sea with its angular waves recalling running animals. ... She feels against her the little warm being pressing against her chest, wanting to live."

M

Maghreb: n. Setting Sun in Arabic. Name for the area that now is made of Morocco or North Africa. Maghreb[i]an (adj.)

Maquis: Thick underbrush in some of the southern hills of France used by the French underground during World War Two.

Merlin: Legendary medieval wizard. Here, the magician is a symbolic portal to escapism.

Mistral: Powerful recurring wind in Provence with innumerable references in music, literature and folklore.

Musset, Alfred (de): Nineteenth Century playwright and poet who captured the impact of love and passion on the soul.

O

O'Neil, Eugene: Reference to the playwright's family house near the beaches in New London, Connecticut.

P

Pavlovian: adj. After the researcher Ivan Pavlov interested in conditioned reaction to stimuli.

Pharaonic [laws]: Reference in this work to the powerful cinematographic [if not verifiably biblical] edict by the [a] Pharaoh of Egypt to ban the very mention of Moses.

Pointe Rouge: Beach to the east of Marseille.

Primo Levi: Writer and survivor of the concentration camps.

Prodigal: Iconic son having left his home returns tearfully for forgiveness. In this instance, the absence [for military duty] was imposed on the son.

Q

Quasimodo: The 'malformed' hunchback of Victor Hugo's Notre Dame de Paris. The novelist captures the ambivalence between Quasimodo's grotesque appearance and his tenderness towards Esmeralda.

R

Rembrandt: Painting of the married Bathsheba with a faraway ambivalent glance in her eyes as she reads a love note from King David.

Renoir, Pierre-Auguste (1841–1919): was a French artist who was a leading painter in the development of the Impressionist style. The poem "Light and Flesh" is about Andrée, his last model and muse before his death.

Rockwell, Norman: Iconic realistic painter of a reputed idealized vision of American history. His museum contains striking, lesser known studies of the civil rights struggle.

Ronsard, Pierre (de): French poet of the Renaissance: Known for his refined odes to love: one of the best remembered makes a reference to the ephemeral beauty of a rose.

S

Semprùn, Jorge: Franco-Spanish writer and survivor of the concentration camps. In essence in Literature or Life equates writing with some sort of survival.

Senghor, Léopold Sédar: Belated recognition on my part of an important influence in my studies of this poet and politician from Sénégal. One of the most central African intellectual of the twentieth century, in particular in poems like "Femme noire" [see below], "Neige sur Paris "and "À New York," where he lyrically paints his feelings living in multiple cultures.

Femme noire

Femme nue, femme noire
Vêtue de ta couleur qui est vie, de ta forme qui est beauté
J'ai grandi à ton ombre; la douceur de tes mains bandait mes yeux
Et voilà qu'au cœur de l'Eté et de Midi,
Je te découvre, Terre promise, du haut d'un haut col calciné
Et ta beauté me foudroie en plein cœur, comme l'éclair d'un aigle

Femme nue, femme obscure
Fruit mûr à la chair ferme, sombres extases du vin noir, bouche qui fais lyrique ma bouche
Savane aux horizons purs, savane qui frémis aux caresses ferventes du Vent d'Est
Tamtam sculpté, tamtam tendu qui gronde sous les doigts du vainqueur
Ta voix grave de contralto est le chant spirituel de l'Aimée

Femme noire, femme obscure
Huile que ne ride nul souffle, huile calme aux flancs de l'athlète, aux flancs des princes du Mali
Gazelle aux attaches célestes, les perles sont étoiles sur la nuit de ta peau.

Délices des jeux de l'Esprit, les reflets de l'or ronge ta peau qui se moire

A l'ombre de ta chevelure, s'éclaire mon angoisse aux soleils prochains de tes yeux.

Femme nue, femme noire
Je chante ta beauté qui passe, forme que je fixe dans l'Eternel
Avant que le destin jaloux ne te réduise en cendres pour nourrir les racines de la vie.

Léopold Sédar Senghor, Chants d'ombre

Stations of the Cross: The use of this reference in this case is the way the family pictures in the hallway of this man's house resembled the memories of the various stages of his life.

Stendhal: see The Happy few.

Synesthesia: Literary terminology and technique referring to the reference, overlapping and cross-affecting of human senses such as visual stimulus to smell, hearing to colors, etc....

T

Thames River: Long Island inlet into the city of New London, Connecticut.

The Happy Few: Expression used in the original English by the French writer Stendhal (Marie-Henri Beyle). Stendhal would regularly dedicate his books to "The Happy Few" by which he meant the few readers who would really capture the meaning and tone of his writings: Used a little more expansively in the poem.

Trompe l'oeil: Painting technique that 'fools' the observer into believing the scene [persons looking down from a balcony] is real.

V

Vandals: Germanic tribes that contributed to the Fall of Rome. In this case, pointing out that Rome still existed afterwards, which would not be necessarily the case for the stored electronic data.

Vigny, Alfred de: French Nineteenth century Romantic playwright, poet and politician.

W

Wertmüller, Lina: One of the early woman movie director and writer. Her *Seven Beauties* (Italian 1975) movie in particular.

Index

A certain pride still on display,	*24*
A friendly slap on the back.	*25*
A Good Start	**59**
Abnormal in a Normal World	**67**
Abstraction	**12**
Africa	**69**
Akin to voyeuristic tourism	*57*
Amplification	**43**
An Eternal Second	**93**
Androgynous undercurrent of sexuality.	*21*
Anonymously shielded by the vagaries of military roulette-wheel:	*44*
Another gadget. Another timid step...	*36*
Antithesis:	*64*
At the center of everything:	*22*
Avatar	**83**
Awkward mindless re-adjustment of salt and pepper shakers...	*39*
Barnyard Noises	**16**
Beautiful Ship	**80**
Beethoven's Universe	**11**
Bluish Marble	**35**
Bothersome echoes,	*115*
Bright of mind... Short of stature.	*18*
Candide (Revisited)	**62**
Carnal flagrance vaporized into eternal seconds	*87*
Cinecittà	**6**
Circular setting of death and dying.	*48*
Cold Indifference	**23**
Compartmentalization	**70**
Contended high priests, on high bench, on high court	*60*

Cosmic singularity of her features.	*93*
Counter Currents	**110**
Crime and victim. Blood and flesh:	*71*
Crystalline world of Mediterranean beginnings.	*50*
Custer's Last Stand	**55**
Daily rounds to appropriately sized tiny house:	*43*
Darken world of unreeling pops and hisses.	*2*
Daydreams	*33*
Denied	**41**
Different Endings	**46**
Digitized Débris	**84**
Displayed noodle soup results	*47*
Dreamscape	**57**
Dying Tendrils	**24**
En poussière	**103**
Essences of petals. Extracts of sunlight.	*7*
Evil walls of physical and moral rectitude.	*70*
Evils of twisted minds and times:	*6*
Exquisite intelligence of sarcastic retort to sly comment:	*110*
Façonner le futur	**109**
Fading bluish letters on the truck:	*82*
Favorite one-eyed teddy bear	*41*
Feats wrapped in capes of colorful daring.	*89*
Fragrance charnelle volatilisée en secondes éternelles	*88*
From on high,	*37*
Games. Expansion of youthful energy	*46*
Gods and Codes	**50**
Google Earth and Heartbreak	**36**
He already had his war paint applied by sunrise.	*55*
He had discovered in himself the talent to transform grammar	*108*
He had wished for proof, as he had long suspected,	*105*
He saw the whole edifice... Precious and indestructible,	*101*
Hellish centrifugal forces of the camps	*78*
Hellish domestic disturbance:	*51*
Holiday Meal Chemistry	**14**

Humanity tries to decipher knowledge	*13*
I've Got to Die Like Sinatra	**20**
ICU	**48**
Ideals and Fairytales	**61**
Il existe un chemin près de Marseille.	*9*
Il regarda l'édifice entier... Précieux et indestructible...	*103*
Il s'était découvert le talent de transformer la grammaire	*109*
Immortal Embers	**113**
Incongruous warmth on his nape... In ice storm.	*111*
Inconvenient	**42**
Indice aimé	**88**
Infliction of sadistic treatment properly shared	
as proper family member:	*67*
Into Dust	**101**
Ironically feeling like a forced-fed goose:	*63*
It had been such a long time... since they had seen each other.	*106*
James Dean's Tee Shirt	**4**
Jumble of fallen trees and confusion of guttural groans.	*59*
Knowing too Much	**22**
L'effet d'un papillon	**112**
La dentelle	**107**
Lace	**106**
Layered sheets of brittle lithium whiteness	*12*
Le beau navire	**81**
Lessons to be learned and wisdom to be gathered	*16*
Life born out of the hopeful maternal grimace	*68*
Light and Flesh	**118**
Longtemps... qu'ils ne s'étaient revus.	*107*
Lost... The immediacy of timelessness:	*92*
Love Molecule	**85**
Loved Trait	**87**
Men and Moths	**90**
Molecular relationships and atomic-size egos.	*27*
Mont Sainte-Victoire (English)	**10**
Mont Sainte-Victoire (French)	**9**

Multi-layered confusion of pubescence: *31*
Muscular arms shaped for the glare of media violence.   *91*
Mythologie paternelle mouillée associée à celle marine.   *81*

Natural Laws and Gods   **56**
Needs and events sprinkled in the landscape of the mundane,   *85*
No Longer of his World   **89**
Nobility in the inner simplicity of actions   *45*
Not Forgotten   **96**
Not much idealism left unscathed   *61*
Number 17451   **78**

Obscenity   **73**
Of Guano and Human Progress   **64**
Of Instinctive Nurturing   **68**
Of Purple Rain and Other Things   **21**
Off the side of the road and far from kindness,   *15*
On the slippery riverbank of paleontological muds,   *69*
Once again,   *34*
Once in one's life, a name develops to mean... Breathing.   *96*
Once Upon a Time... in the Future   **27**
One Size Fits All   **60**
Oneness of drenched paternal mythology   *80*
Out-of-body experience...   *4*

Parallels   **105**
Past Third and Going Home   **53**
Patches of Meaning   **45**
Pâté de campagne and Laissez-faire   **63**
Pavlovian Sounds   **66**
Priorities   **47**
Properly Scented Rabbit Pâté.   *28*
Provence : l'Arlésienne Suite, Farandole et Carillon   **7**
Public apparitions: *17*

Real obscenity: this one non-verbalized.   *73*
Reparations: Camus and Capital Punishment   **71**
Replaced   **44**
Rich diversity of girls from resulting american melting pot.   *53*

Saint Martin and the Donkey	13
Seemingly flat world of photographic stillness.	11
Seemingly unforced innate fluidity.	20
Seismic aftershocks	96
Shaping the Future	108
Sightless Images	92
Singed wings and crackling snaps of dying life.	90
Singularité cosmique de son visage.	95
Slow Dancing	31
Small Things	19
Smells of success.	62
Smirks of disapproval from the rightist corner of the clan	14
Solid directions from flimsy fumes of convictions	56
Sounds of Silence in the Kitchen	39
Sparkles in a human mind	23
Splendid Fragility	76
Splendid fragility of the cadence of words,	76
Still... That omnipresent sheen of style and posture	83
Stones set into the humid earth,	65
Strange... the malleable distance between right and wrong:	66
Sulfurous clouds from the fissures of Hades.	118
Surprise!	17
Swirls of unbridled violence done to body parts	42
Temerity	75
That snake had been there all the while	29
The Beagle and the Kitten	15
The Boxer and the Sparrow	91
The Cathedral and the Meter Maid	28
The Effect of a Butterfly	111
The End of Everything	37
The End of Simplicity	100
The Ice Cream Truck	82
The Life of a Bubble	115
The Name That Must Not Be Said	98
The Pyramid Builder II	65
The very banality of his spot on the calendar,	75
There is a path near Marseille.	10
They used to be members of the nobility of old feelings:	84
This Side of Illusion	2

Tiédeur incongrue sur la nuque... Sous une pluie gelée.	*112*
Total Recall	**38**
Turing's Cathedral: Lost Paradise	**29**
Une seconde éternelle	**95**
University Bull Sessions and the Universe	**25**
Unlike the oscillations of well-behaved photons,	*113*
Unquestioned beliefs in the true heading of the maternal star.	*100*
Verbal Architecture of Past Happiness	**34**
Warm Sand	**33**
Wishing Otherwise	**18**
Wisps of prairie-green gentleness.	*35*
Wizardly of blinking lights. Alchemy of futuristic potions.	*38*
Wrought iron chairs and tables:	*19*
Yellow Lights	**51**

ABOUT THE AUTHOR

Jean-Yves Solinga

Jean-Yves was born in Algeria, of French parents, moving to Morocco as a babe in mother's arms when his father was transferred to Salé: practically across from the Kasbah des Udayas of Rabat. Thereafter, he spent an idyllic youth between Morocco and Southern France. Upon settling in America with his family, at the age of 15, he soon began writing poetry as a teenager: being first published in *A Letter Among Friends* along with John Norman of New London, CT. After leaving College, Jean-Yves began a successful career in teaching and lecturing. He holds a doctorate in French on the representation of the Maghrebian [North African] landscape found in the texts by Pierre Loti, André Gide, Albert Camus and Jean-Marie Le Clézio.

Since his retirement he has published several books of poetry: *Clair-Obscur of the Soul* (2008), *Clair-obscur de l'âme* [in French] (2008), *In the Shade of a Flower* (2009), *Landscape of Envies* (2010), *Words Made of Silk* (2011). His books offer a singularly unique view of mankind's reflection through the prism of the lyrical language and the quasi impressionist imagery of his poetry. "At times, some passages are examples of the translation of the human condition into pure thought" writes Michael Linnard.

He has been a featured speaker at the Alliance Française of New Haven and Hartford. Presented at the Center of the Teaching of French at Yale University and Southern Connecticut State University on the use of poetry in language studies. Published in "*Art et poésie*" edited by the renowned French poet Jean-Claude George. He has read at the Poetry

Institute of New Haven, Wesleyan University book store, the Cantab Lounge in Cambridage, the Blue Star Café in Providence, the Guilford Green Barn. He has featured at the Arts café in Mystic, the Hygienics, the Bean and leaf, the Bank Square Bookstore. He has co-featured at the Mystic Art Gallery, and at the Harriet Beecher Stowe Center on the theme of social justice in poetry. Jean-Yves has had poems published by the *Free Poet Collective Ekpharsis Project* at the New Britain museum, the *Ekpharsis Loft Anthology* of Providence and the *Little Red Tree Anthology*. His poetry has been nominated three times for a Pushcart Award.

Jean-Yves Solinga is a poet of immense ability and range whose poetry is truly remarkable. It contains many breathtakingly beautiful and sophisticated poems that reach out to the very limits of the human condition where true art exists. Many facets of his work find inspiration and perspective in his cultural duality. This gives his poems an historical and critical breath.

In *Impressions of Reality* Jean-Yves continues to search, as did Montaigne, into the individual experience for something beyond the biographic or the particular: towards the universal. His, are poems that transcend the personal experience. His themes and images go into the elements of the contingent and accidental to find the eternally repeated and repeatable human moments.

Photograph taken by: Katie Norman

www.ingramcontent.com/pod-product-compliance
Lightning Source LLC
Chambersburg PA
CBHW080513110426
42742CB00017B/3093